Ears of the Angels

Ears of the Angels

Healing the Sounds—Heard and Unheard— of Humans and Animals

PART I. CLOSER TO THE MUSIC

A not-always-graceful journey to telepathic sound transformation

❦

By Deena Zalkind Spear
Illustrations and Cover Art by Bruce Burgess
Cartoons by Deena Spear
Cartoons by Robert Spear

Part II *(Working in the World of Matter – A violin maker's acoustics manual with a subtle slide toward the fourth dimension)* is available only in the hardcover edition (ISBN 0-9712173-0-0) published by Singing Woods Press. It may be purchased through the author's website **www.singing-woods.org** or call (607) 387-8488 for information.

The hardcover edition of this book (ISBN 0-9712173-0-0) includes both Parts I and II. It is published by Singing Woods Press and can be purchased online at **www.singing-woods.org** or call (607) 387-8488 for information.

Published and distributed in the United States by: Hay House, Inc., P.O. Box 5100, Carlsbad, CA 92018-5100 • *Phone:* (760) 431-7695 or (800) 654-5126 • *Fax:* (760) 431-6948 or (800) 650-5115 • www.hayhouse.com • *Published and distributed in Australia by:* Hay House Australia Pty Ltd, 18/36 Ralph St., Alexandria NSW 2015 • *Phone:* 612-9669-4299 • *Fax:* 612-9669-4144 • *e-mail:* info@hayhouse.com.au • *Published and Distributed in the United Kingdom by:* Hay House UK, Ltd. • Unit 202, Canalot Studios • 222 Kensal Rd., London W10 5BN • *Phone:* 020-8962-1230 • *Fax:* 020-8962-1239 • *Distributed in Canada by:* Raincoast • 9050 Shaughnessy St., Vancouver, B.C. V6P 6E5 • *Phone:* (604) 323-7100 • *Fax:* (604) 323-2600

Graphic design and layout by: Torri Bennington, West Hill Graphics, Inc., Ithaca, NY

Library of Congress Control Number: 2002110938

ISBN 1-4019-0187-5

06   05   04   03   4   3   2   1
1st Hay House printing, May 2003

Printed in the United States of America

left to right: Pocca, Deena, and Yuppee Dupp

eena Spear was graduated from Cornell University in 1971 with a degree in neurobiology. She worked as a chemical analyst for several years and trained as a violin maker, becoming a full-time luthier by the mid 1970s. She is also a 1997 graduate of Barbara Brennan Healing Science Training. Deena combines her education and experience in biological science, violin making, and energy healing to alter sound vibrations of musical instruments and sentient beings. She lives in Ithaca, New York with her violin maker/writer/residential designer husband, Bob, and canine companions H. Yuppington Duppsworth (Yuppee Dupp) and Poccata in B (Pocca).

This book is dedicated to my parents:

Albert M. Zalkind (1910–1995)
For his great love and incredible humor, and for
staying close by even after departing physical reality.

Ruth Laster Zalkind (1915–2000)
For her belief that I must be doing something real
even if it made no logical sense to her.

TABLE OF CONTENTS

PART I. CLOSER TO THE MUSIC
A not-always-graceful journey to telepathic sound transformation

PART II. WORKING IN THE WORLD OF MATTER

A violin maker's acoustics manual with a subtle slide toward the fourth dimension

Part II is available only in the hardcover edition (ISBN 0-9712173-0-0) published by Singing Woods Press. It may be purchased through the author's website **www.singing-woods.org** or call (607) 387-8488 for information.

Ears of the Angels

The usually "Upside-down" Pocca!

ACKNOWLEDGEMENTS

I would like to thank my husband, Robert J. Spear, for his comma relocation program. While an exact comma census was not taken, I believe that not a single life was lost. His other sensitive editing such as pointing out the need to release some sentences from their tortured state, or the joy of a more liberal use of paragraphs, was also greatly appreciated.

I also wish to thank Alexander Thornhill for reading each and every word as it emerged from my computer, for tech support even at 1:00 a.m., and for always being there to fix my computer when it ate my book, ate my e-mail, and begged to be taken for recycling. As I write this—in longhand—just weeks from actual book printing, my computer has made one last dramatic attempt at retirement by pretending the entire book files do not exist. Alex thought he was through with this book. Oh Alex . . .

I am very grateful to Marianne Alexander who, through the miracle of e-mail, also read every word of every version within a day of its birth. Her enthusiasm and support helped get me through this project. (Not to mention the hours of giggling after she said to me, "Deena, in the 30 years I've known you, you have gone from absolute moron to genius. What that has done for me is that I will never again consider someone hopeless. If you can do it, anyone can do it.")

I want to thank Philip Pan for his exceptional foreword as well as all my wonderful friends and clients who made the time to write their experiences for this book. Thanks also to Bruce Burgess for his beautiful illustrations. My appreciation to Joyce Burgess, both for her manuscript reading and for explaining to her talented artist son, Bruce, the nature of physical time. I also want to thank Durga Jacobs-Bor, Carol Kulig, Marianne Alexander, Amy Painter, Tom King, Jill King, and Ingrid Cantarella Fox for corrections and suggestions. My thanks to Bonnie Cohen for her comments on text and titles and to June Fritchman for final copy-editing.

My appreciation also to Sandra Levy, who trusted and assisted my healing endeavors from the start, and to her dear, late husband, Richard, who valued my work and made me laugh when he said to me: "Deena, unorthodox is too mild a word for what you do." I miss you, Richard.

My gratitude to all those who have assisted me along my path over the years including Marlene Sandler, teacher, mentor, and friend; Carla Gordan, teacher of the heart; Louise

Cook, for her friendship and intuitive gifts; Roberta Herzog, intuitive and friend; Karl Roy, violin master teacher; and Carleen Hutchins, violin acoustician and innovator. I wish to express gratitude to Barbara Brennan and the teachers at the Barbara Brennan School of Healing who assisted me, as well as Shelby Hammit for her "Energy Anatomy" course. To those who wrote letters in support of me and the book—Alan Cohen, Jill Lawrence, Janie Emerson, Amy Painter (and Elvie), my thanks. My gratitude also to Laurie Conrad, Gerda Swearingen, and Carol Kulig for their support, and to Sheezava for inspiration.

My appreciation to Terri Diener for keeping me in communication with my dog, Yuppee Dupp, whose creative agenda rarely included sitting around watching me type this book. My thanks to Yuppee Dupp for keeping me company when I wasn't doing something he considered boring, and for loving me unconditionally. My thanks to the lovely and usually upside-down Pocca for waiting until I had just finished the main manuscript of this book before making her grand appearance in her puppy costume, ready to snuggle anytime she wasn't trying to consume the contents of the refrigerator.

My gratitude also to Gary Frisch for always being up for violin experiments even though he had to drive back and forth over The Woodrow Wilson Bridge. Also my appreciation to George Bissinger for bringing his equipment to D.C. and measuring some of those experiments.

My thanks to Torri Bennington for her elegant graphics work and extraordinary patience. Thank you to Leigh Dezelan for graphics assistance. My appreciation to photographer Barry Perlus for consultation on artwork reproduction and to Joe Sepe of Pioneer Printing in Lodi, New York, as well as Dick and Jody Reynolds of Reynolds Book Bindery in Binghamton, New York, for printing consultation. My gratitude to Norine V. Grzesik-Rathbone for house and portrait photographs, and thank you to Allen Walls and Gail Birnbaum for publishing advice. My special thanks to Amy Opperman Cash and Paul Cash for essential publishing assistance.

My thanks also to all my friends who have supported me over the years who are not named here (except for Irene Brown, whom I will name here in appreciation for more than three decades of being there for me). Thank you to those who have written endorsements for this book, old friends and new. Finally, my gratitude to Dr. Christiane Northrup for her sense of humor and her belief in me.

FOREWORD

I have had something to say through the violin since I squawked out my first tune at age eight. With the blessings of supportive parents, great teachers and a strong work ethic, I churned my way through the Juilliard School, through recitals, competitions, and auditions to where I am today. As the concertmaster of a professional orchestra, recitalist, and soloist, I make a decent living while pursuing that same lifelong goal—to put bow to string and have the violin say what I want it to. *Through the violin . . .* this is where Deena Spear enters the picture.

Equipment is no small part of any musician's career, and, for a string player, it is often a disproportionately large financial commitment. I know of few other occupations where from one to four years of gross salary are consumed, out of pocket, by one's primary and essential tool of the trade. The quest for the fiddle, which so perfectly melds with its player so as to "play itself," consumes every serious classical string player that I know. This quest leads the musician from shop to shop in search of not only the right instrument within one's budget, but the right *luthier* to enable that instrument to always sound its best.

The ideal musical instrument is an extension of the player's heart and soul. There occurs a magical shortcut, which seems to bypass the ardors and complexities of technique, and the music simply flows from the artist through the instrument and to the listeners. Of course, proper training and preparation play a large role in this, but no amount of practice can fully capture the synergy of a great performer mated to his or her ideal instrument. Before working with Deena, I had resigned myself to the idea that only the lucky few who could somehow come into possession of a legendary Old Italian violin could achieve this synergy. The rest of us would have to settle for good, but second-rate fiddles. We would therefore also have to settle for a certain plateau in our abilities to express ourselves through music. On hindsight, this was an unnecessary and potentially tragic conclusion.

My current violin, an 1837 Auguste Bernardel, captured my heart the first time I belted out a few notes on its G string. The D was pretty good, the A a bit nasal, and the E positively shrieked. I decided I would "compensate" for the shortcomings of over 75% of the instrument's range; I had to have that G string! The very reputable dealer assured me that they could adjust it to meet my desires. They couldn't.

I decided to go ahead with the purchase because I had become familiar with the unique acoustical tuning skills of Deena Spear. Since first hearing the dramatic change her techniques had brought to a colleague's cello, I had become fascinated by her unconventional approach and sometimes spectacular results. I read and understood the techniques she published in a trade journal. They were different, cutting edge, and they made sense. More than that, my own ears heard her make dull instruments come alive. My previous experiences with even the most highly-regarded *luthiers* amounted to limited degrees of success achieved by their tapping the fiddle's soundpost here and there. Over the years, I discovered that I was pretty much as good a soundpost-tapper as any of them. But Deena was something new, and she gave me enough hope to commit $40,000 to an instrument that actually made me wince in its upper two octaves.

Ten years later, I can say that not only was my confidence well-placed, but that Deena and the Bernardel have literally exceeded my wildest dreams. This is not the same violin I bought in 1991. It looks the same, but its personality, its playability, its power, and its very soul have not just been improved, they have been transformed. And, more importantly, the transformation has paralleled my own growth as a player and artist. The more I sought to strip my playing of undue effort and over-thinking, the more I sought to breathe through and with the violin, the more Deena and the Bernadel have evolved along with me. I now have not only a great violin; I have a great violin "custom-tuned" to me! It has become more than just an instrument—it has become my teacher.

Deena's evolution is the story of *Ears of the Angels*, the story of how she followed her dreams as a violin maker along a remarkably different path. If it were a work of fiction, readers would enjoy it for its humor, its imagination, and for its ability to successfully draw one into the esoteric intricacies of the fine art of violin making. In short, it's a good read, whether you believe it or not. Having observed and benefited from her techniques as they progressed from the novel to the truly metaphysical, I have been incrementally indoctrinated into the Spear approach to acoustical tuning. First, it was in the comfortable realm of the physical: little bits of clay stuck to the sides of the instruments; minuscule crumbs of wood scraped off the insides; invisible shavings from the *f* holes. Then, it started getting a little strange: Deena changing the instrument's sound by simply tapping and holding it for a few minutes; Deena repairing an unglued seam without any glue; Deena adjusting the instrument to respond despite the onset of Florida's summer humidity *while on the telephone to me from her home in Maryland.*

It all worked. I heard it. So did my family and colleagues and audience.

I have had to conclude that the laws of physics, as commonly accepted in the scientific community, are severely limited and insufficient to explain reality as I have observed it. As a violinist, I don't care—the fiddle just keeps sounding better and better. As a human being, I can't help but be more than a little curious as to what forces are at work here. There are a great many things in life that I don't understand and can't significantly control. Some are horrible, like inhumanity, insanity, and war. Others, like a Baryshnikov pirouette or a Bach fugue, are so compelling in their beauty that they push us to seek to demystify them in the hopes that we may have more of them to enjoy. *"How do they do that?"* is a question very much worth asking, even if there are no answers at this time. And so, I hope you will ask the question, *"How does Deena do that?"* even if you are thoroughly convinced that there are no answers.

However she does it, I and many others certainly hope she will continue to do it and also pass her skills on to others. What she does for musical instruments and their owners is unique and invaluable; what she may do to expand the boundaries of human ability may be even more valuable. I have been privileged to have walked with Deena along significant parts of her journey, and it is an adventure I look forward to continuing. I invite you join us by taking an honest look at the path she has walked so far.

It's been weird, wacky, fun, rewarding, and beautiful. What more could you ask for?

Philip D. Pan
B.M., M.M., the Juilliard School
Concertmaster, Jacksonville Symphony Orchestra

Creating harmony of vibration

PREFACE

If it vibrates, it can be tuned. Everything is energy—violins, animals, people, potato chips, thoughts, feelings, and events. They all vibrate.

After many years of working as a professional violin maker, I felt drawn to attend a four-year energy healing school. I also pursued additional assistance privately with a gifted and adventurous mentor. When I entered the school, I had no idea that as my healing abilities unfolded they would, or could, be used to change the sound of violins with my mind and my heart. The talents that have emerged are ones I would not have considered possible if I had thought of them beforehand, which I hadn't.

Part I, *Closer to the Music,* is the story of how I learned to bring about more harmony of vibration, first using innovative physical methods on violins, violas, and cellos to alter acoustics, and, ultimately, using telepathic energy to adjust the audible and inaudible sound of instruments *and* sentient beings.

Thanks to my experience of using energy to enhance the sound of bowed string instruments, where I had the opportunity to hear acoustical transformation with my physical ears, when I performed healing work on humans and animals I had more confidence that I could help create beauty of sound that is not in our usual range of auditory perception. Whether tuning the unheard resonance of a chemical toxin to lessen or eliminate its damaging effects on the body, or encouraging a return to harmony from the dissonance of toxic emotion, for me it is all similar to telepathically adjusting an instrument. Part I includes many examples of healings that resulted from changing the "silent" sound of people and animals. The majority of these sessions took place long distance. In some cases, my clients have contributed their perspectives for this book.

As the instruments were teaching me that I really *was* altering resonance with thought, I learned to recognize acoustical transformation with an inner sense—a kind of "felt" sound. Healing is creating more harmony of vibration in multiple dimensions of the body and the spirit. The most important listening I do is with the "Ears of the Angels."

Part II, *Working in the World of Matter,* is available only in the hardcover edition (ISBN 0-9712173-0-0) published by Singing Woods Press and may be purchased online through my website at www.singing-woods.org or call (607) 387-8488 for information. It is a detailed description of those innovative *PHYSICAL* methods I developed for changing the quality and carrying power of violins, violas, and cellos. These were important steps for me on the path to developing telepathic sound-tuning skills.

I feel compelled both to publish and teach this new violin acoustics information so that it is not lost. It greatly expands the known methods of enhancing the sound of bowed string instruments and can be learned by a patient craftsman, even if he or she does not aspire to consciously work as an energy healer. Because these techniques become increasingly more subtle as one progresses, they can also be used as steppingstones to changing sound with thought and love—the source of the music.

D.Z.S.
Ithaca, New York

INTRODUCTION

I was six months out of college and furiously preparing for the medical boards, entrance exams required to apply for medical school. I had been studying for months, and the tests were two weeks away. It was then I realized that I just couldn't do it. Yes, I was interested in health and healing. And I was learning that the thoughts and beliefs of the person had far more to do with illness and recovery than was currently accepted by the medical community. I didn't think my future patients would believe me. I didn't want to spend years learning about drugs. So that was that. I wouldn't do it.

My father was anything but pleased.

Cast adrift, I began looking for something else to do with my life. My friend Marianne, a Suzuki cello teacher at the time, showed me how to play "Twinkle Twinkle Little Star" on the violin. Something happened to me. It was nothing rational, but suddenly I became obsessed. I had to learn about the violin. I was not overqualified for the job. I had a degree in neurobiology from Cornell University, had studied piano while growing up, and had attained a good solid level of mediocrity as a musician—except for sight reading, which I couldn't do at all. And I couldn't count time either. Otherwise, I could "Für Elise" away as well as any other not particularly talented kid.

So at age 22 I bought a violin and started to take lessons. It was clear that even after any number of years of study, I would never approach the heights of mediocrity to which I had risen on the piano. But I was still obsessed with the violin.

Since I had lots of art training, both in drawing and clay sculpture, I thought perhaps I could work with my hands. Of course I'd never done any woodworking. I had never even held a file and didn't know it cut in only one direction. (In my day, only boys were allowed to take wood shop, while girls were required to sit through home economics classes—it didn't take— anyone coming to visit me brings dinner.)

I had a vague idea of some of the other hand tools—very vague. I had never actually touched any of them. In fact, the only woodworking tool I'd handled was a carpenter's framing hammer. These are not normally used in violin making, although I have seen a distraught violin maker threaten his violin with one.

I learned from the local guitar shop (I played a bit of folk guitar, badly) that the man who conducted the local high school orchestra also had a violin shop he ran part-time in the evenings. I located his telephone number and called him. I asked if I could come watch, or learn or something. Anything. "No," he said.

We were married four years later.

But I am getting ahead of myself.

My husband to be, Robert Spear, gave me some excuse about not being trained enough to help anyone else. I figured anything he knew was more than I knew, which was quite true. Furthermore, I spring from a line of lawyers on my father's side, and a mother who should have been one. I persisted. Bob was going off to study in the summer with Karl Roy, the headmaster of the Bavarian State School of Violin Making. The classes were being held at a United States university. He guessed that after he returned, I could come to his little shop. Whew. My whole future was hanging in the balance. So was his. Who knew? Perhaps our guardian angels gave him a whack with an etheric 2x4. Or perhaps I, too, would have been a good lawyer.

I waited out the summer and then went tripping down to his shop, a windowless interior room in a converted old school. There we were, me in my granny dress and he in his polyester pants. ("At least they weren't plaid," he commented when he read this.) What a pair. Neither of us knew what to make of the other. But I wanted to learn violin work. He agreed and proceeded to show me how to plug up little holes in violin pegs.

When the pegs became worn and had moved too far into the violin, new holes for the strings were needed, so we plugged the old ones. This is something I wouldn't bother to do now. I was all enthusiasm without a shred of skill. He handed me a file and told me it cut only on the push stroke. I was off and, uh, limping—making small piles of ebony dust and tiny useless pieces of ebony that fit nothing.

That same year, 1974, I started to travel to Montclair, New Jersey to study with Carleen Maley Hutchins. She was doing innovative work with violin acoustics. I was still struggling with the basics, but at that time she had classes for everyone. Bob continued to study in the summers with Karl Roy.

Nearly four years later, we joined one another's classes and began to wonder where our relationship was going. Duh. Bob calls it love at last sight. We were married in 1977. We spent the first week of our honeymoon trying to sharpen our scroll-cutting gouges on a grinder set up in the New Hampshire woods, where Carleen had graciously loaned us the use of a cottage.

The rest of the honeymoon was spent in Karl Roy's classes at the University of New Hampshire. We worked from eight in the morning until well past midnight seven days a week for several weeks. The un-airconditioned dorms at the university had small single beds, which our room could only accommodate by putting the head of one at the foot of the other. The mattresses were coated in plastic and the sheets never stayed on for more than 10 minutes. It was so hot the only way I could fall asleep was to wrap myself in a wet sheet. Ah romance. I guess it was visiting someone else.

I retired my granny dresses. Bob released his polyester pants—after making sure they could feed themselves—to the wilds of the Salvation Army. My mother was thrilled that I was marrying someone with a real job. He quit his high school teaching job not too long after that. We wanted to do violin work full time. Now there was that romance, but unfortunately not much money.

I couldn't convince my husband that given our intermittent income it was important to pay the bills in the order in which things were cut off, not the order in which the bills arrived. It didn't fit his sense of organization. By agreement, I then took over the payments due, over-due, way overdue, and collection agency due. It saved years of arguments, and we almost always had electricity and a working phone.

With that issue resolved, most of our disagreements in those early years were confined to such topics as violin purfling, the black and white inlay that goes around the edge of the violin. Is that an improvement upon a fight about which way to put a roll of toilet paper, or the direction the tines of a fork should face in the drain board—up, where they can stab someone, or down, where they collect bacteria? It quickly became clear to us that if someone bothered to put the toilet paper in the holder at all—be happy. And if someone managed to do the dishes, fork tine and knife direction authority would be conveyed to him or her. Purfling was another matter.

Over the years we managed to achieve a reputation in our craft. Some of it is even very good—if you find the right people to talk to. Those people may become fewer in number, given my current activities and the publication of this book.

We each have made our own instruments. As I began to focus more of my attention on sound, my husband bravely allowed me to do the set-up and final acoustical adjustment on all of his instruments. Eventually, I asked him to do some of the early work on my violins, for example, joining the boards for the top and back. When he looked particularly agreeable I asked him to put in the pegs, as they like him better.

We now have instruments with professional musicians around the country. My husband has made cellos for Mstislav Rostropovich and John Martin, who had not yet retired as principal cellist for the National Symphony Orchestra in Washington, D.C. There was not a causal relationship between John's obtaining a Spear cello and his retirement, as far as we know. Since he had been principal cellist there for about 45 years, he probably had earned the right to watch the traffic on the television set from the comfort of his living room.

I wanted to learn how to better adjust sound. This forced me to go beyond traditional violin-making knowledge and spend years developing completely new methods for balancing the vibrations. Some of it included making scrapers with which to reach inside the instruments and remove small amounts of wood from just the right spots. Before I became practiced at my innovative techniques, some instruments took days to adjust. Although the changes to sound were well worth the trouble, my poor musician friends often took on a glazed-over look after hours of one of these sessions.

After two decades of focusing on little but violin making and violin acoustics, I noticed a book on the shelf in a bookstore. The book was titled *Hands of Light* and was written by Barbara Ann Brennan. I'd always been interested in things metaphysical; in the early 70s I had read *The Autobiography of a Yogi* and some Edgar Cayce books.

I had also attended Jane Roberts' classes. Jane was an intuitive who wrote a number of books on the nature of reality and how we create it. She was the first trance medium I had ever experienced, and it was absolutely stunning.

I have since encountered a few good ones and some who weren't even close. One had tricked himself into thinking that he was a genuine medium, complete with a nifty accent, but alas he was not. Then there are those who know they are faking it.

I was most fortunate to start with Jane Roberts, whose talent and integrity were obvious. In her classes, an energy personality, who called himself Seth, spoke through Jane. He was able to correctly tell about things that had not been mentioned to anyone, such as what one had dreamt the night before. It was a clear demonstration of the validity of the medium. ("The medium is the message," he used to quip.) The information that he taught on the nature of reality certainly rearranged my beliefs about how things are, and, because of Seth and Jane, many now see the world very differently.

My interest in the non-physical world was put aside for nearly 20 years as I had only enough time and brain space to be a violin maker. At first this was because I started with knowledge of both violins and woodworking skills in the negative numbers. Then it was because once I finally learned something, I felt compelled to take violin acoustics beyond current knowledge.

But here in front of me was Ms. Brennan's intriguing book. On some of its pages were color pictures of the human auric field. I'd never before seen detailed color paintings of the levels of the energy field surrounding people, which only some can see. It looked fascinating. I put it back on the shelf and walked out of the store. I guess my guide needed to shift from 2x4s to 2x12s. A few weeks later I saw the book again in a different bookstore in a different city. This time I bought it.

After reading some of the book, I looked in the back and noticed information about a school in which Barbara and her staff taught energy healing. Barbara had once been a physicist for NASA. I had always considered myself a psychic brick. Could these skills be taught? The school was holding a three-and-a-half day introductory workshop in our geographic area. I took my psychic-brick self in hand and went to the class.

At one point the instructor had us imagine various colors as we spun energy vortexes on our bodies. I thought I was making it up. Suddenly I became violently nauseated and nearly fainted. As I sank to the floor, I thought, "Wow, this energy stuff is real." A teacher came over and said that I was on the rug feeling so sick because I wasn't grounded and couldn't handle the energy of the exercise. Now I *had* to go to this school. Once again, I was obsessed. (Please note, that is different from possessed—I think.)

I applied to the healing school, was accepted, and began the classes with no clue how they would fit in with violin making. I didn't care at that time; I just knew I had to go. Obsessed, possessed, whatever.

I used to hear rumors about the strange things I did involving innovative physical changes on musical instruments using unusual scraping techniques. Now the truth is far more outrageous than any of the rumors ever were. As I worked my way through the four-year energy healing school, I discovered that I didn't need those scrapers at all. In fact, not only was it much faster to do some of those adjustments mentally, but I learned that there is so much that can be done with violins that has no physical equivalent.

The same is true for people and animals. For example, if you want to remove the energy of an organ donor and instead infuse the recipient's vibrational signature into a transplanted organ to lower (or perhaps eliminate) the dose of antirejection medicine, there is no piece of technical equipment available at any cost that can do the job; but it can be and has been done. It takes a human healer working with energy (see Chapter XVIII—Not Yet Mainstream Medicine).

This is a book about the journey from physical to metaphysical—that sound can be changed dramatically with mental intention and an open heart. It can be changed equally well hands-on or over any physical distance. I routinely help keep my clients' instruments or bodies in better health when they call me on the phone. My clients include concertmasters of symphonies, medical doctors, open-minded people, formerly skeptical people, horses, dogs, cats, and a goldfish. As William Steck, recently retired concertmaster of the National Symphony once said to me, "I don't care how you do it, just so it works."

One fine violinist left my house with a headache. His ears told him that the sound of his violin was changing as I worked on it with my mind alone. That information didn't fit in with his version of reality. It was a painful collision at the intersection of hearing and beliefs.

"Know your audience," I have been told by many of those who heard I was writing a book. Well . . . This book is a somewhat unusual amalgam of topics. It is for those who already know there is more to this world than meets the physical eye. It is for those who don't know there is more to this world and will think me a fruit loop. It is for those who don't care one way or the other, but see that there are innovative methods they can learn about and may use for healing themselves, their animal companions, or their musical instruments. It is for those who might begin the book feeling one way and finish the book with a new view.

"There is no use in trying," said Alice, "one can't believe impossible things."

"I dare say you haven't had much practice," said the Queen. "When I was your age, I always did it for half an hour a day. Why, sometimes I've believed as many as six impossible things before breakfast."

—Lewis Carroll, *Through the Looking Glass*

PART I

Closer to the Music

A not-always-graceful journey
to telepathic sound transformation

Pushing One's Limits

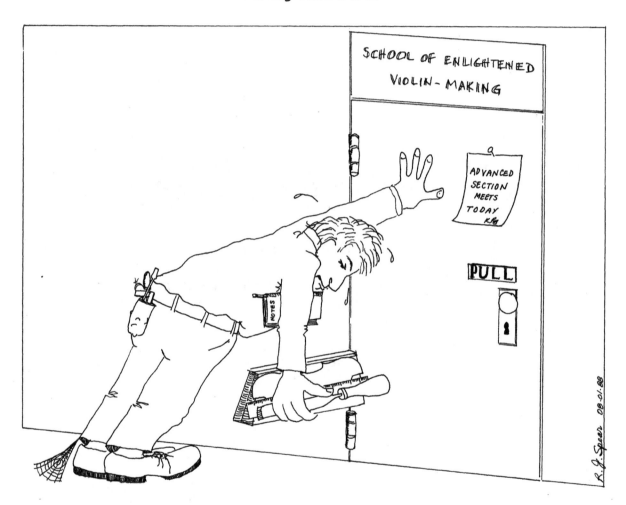

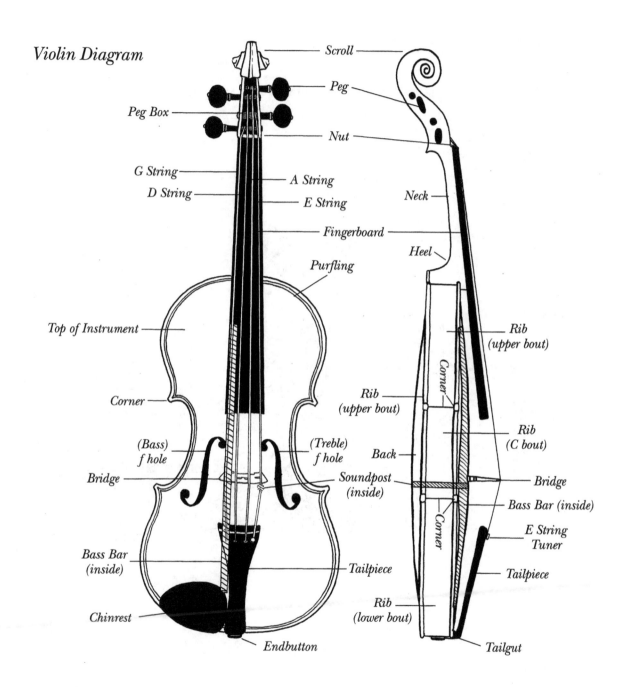

Violin Diagram

Scroll

Peg

Peg Box

Nut

G String

A String

D String

E String

Neck

Fingerboard

Heel

Purfling

Top of Instrument

Rib
(upper bout)

Corner

Corner

Rib
(upper bout)

Rib
(C bout)

(Bass)
f hole

(Treble)
f hole

Back

Bridge

Soundpost
(inside)

Bridge

Bass Bar (inside)

Corner

E String
Tuner

Bass Bar
(inside)

Tailpiece

Tailpiece

Chinrest

Rib
(lower bout)

Endbutton

Tailgut

Taking the learning curve for a spin

CHAPTER I

From Violin to Flower Pot in 150 Hard-to-Repeat Steps

It's a daunting endeavor to try to convey, using black markings on pieces of paper, a part of who you are and what you've learned. I am grateful to others for having done just that. They have helped me enormously. It is important for all of us to do this—to share our experiences and the knowledge gained. Perhaps it is also a responsibility. I don't know. But for the likes of Jane Roberts and her Seth books, and Machaelle Small Wright and her books about her work at Perelandra with devas and nature spirits, I would be much the poorer indeed.

It is now time for me to stop panicking about leaving the security of obscurity. It's time to write about my journey for those who will find the information helpful. With my marketing skills, it may land me in only slightly less obscurity in any case, and all that wonderful panic will have been a complete waste.

The procedures for making innovative physical adjustments to violins are already slipping from my memory as I focus on the energy work. These methods can make dramatic changes to sound, without detectable alterations to the violin body—unlike unfortunate practices, such as regraduation (thinning the wood of the top and back), which violate the integrity of an instrument that was not made by the hand of the one presently performing the work. This ill-conceived removal of wood is all too often executed by desperate repairmen/salesmen who ruin the instruments for all time. Furthermore, as more is learned about set-up acoustics,

I believe that it will become apparent that the thickness of a well-made instrument was frequently never the problem to begin with.

In the early chapters of this book I include a laymen's explanation of the development of my new violin acoustics work. I had always thought that explanations and instructions of my discoveries would be published in a rather dry and stern fashion and available only to a few violin makers and a handful of interested string players. However, it now feels right to include the information here as the foundation for the rest of my story about healing. The more detailed version of the woodworking techniques can be found in Part II of this book. For those who are not interested, Part II may be skipped and it will not go on anyone's permanent record.

My story begins with violins. To many luthiers, the problem with violins is the musicians. It's not enough for their violin, viola, or cello to look beautiful. It's not enough that the maker may have spent many long years learning his craft, aged his expensive quarter-sawn, air-dried European wood for at least a decade or two, and spent hundreds of hours making his work of art with thousands of dollars worth of high-priced imported tools used only for the purpose of making violins. It's not enough that the maker may have suffered enough battle wounds to have bought stock in a band-aid company. Oh no! Those musicians insist that they play an instrument that can soothe the ear, quiet the heart, and fill an entire modern concert hall with sound. Just one little violin, all by its lonesome self. Picky, picky, picky! Well, yes, for many players, their vocation and their avocation are the same. Their finances and their joy depend on it. But aside from that, a musician who can't express himself or herself musically through that little wooden box can get quite cranky indeed.

So, what is a violin maker to do? Why is it that some great soloists might spend a million or two for one of the great Old Italian instruments of the late 1600s or the early 1700s? Is it all those years of playing? Is it something else? That has been the great debate.

From time to time some maker or other claims to have discovered the secret of Stradivari. (Antonio Stradivari and Guarneri Del Gesu are considered to be the greatest of the great master violin makers.) Some think it is in the varnish. One maker grinds up gemstones into his concoction. Others say it is in the soaking of wood. Some even have secret formulas for the broth. We soaked our wood and learned the hard way what happens if you don't change the water. Slime happens. There are some rather nice instruments out there with a big dark stripe down the center of the spruce tops and maple backs, courtesy of the tiny living creatures who bring us slime. Not quite the trademark we had intended. Priceless, decades-old pieces of wood they were. We weren't going to throw them into the wood stove.

Why is it even perceived that there was a secret? Are not the instruments of modern times wonderful enough? That depends on which musician you talk to. But few will reject the opportunity to play their concerts on a Stradivari or Guarneri, or almost any fine Old Italian instrument in good condition.

The situation with bows is similar, only in this case the famous bow makers were the French. A famous old bow could cost tens of thousands of dollars.

During the first years of my new profession, I was not so much concerned with musicians. I was just trying to learn how to produce a beautiful wooden object without slicing an artery. Once I had gotten that far, and I was dealing more frequently with musicians who had instruments of all ages and nationalities, I was rudely rousted out of my comfortable little white silk cocoon to face the music, or rather the lack of it at times.

The problem was that whether an instrument was worth a hundred dollars or a hundred thousand dollars, I was limited in what I could do to change or adjust the sound. There is a soundpost, a small spruce dowel, which stands between the top and back of the violin (viola or cello). It is usually located a few millimeters behind the treble foot of the bridge. The position of this small cylindrical piece can be adjusted using a specially curved metal tool called a soundpost setter. The sound of the instrument changes to some degree as the post is put into slightly different places. These movements are small and generally not more than a millimeter or two at most. One can also play with the age and hardness of the wood in the little dowel, the height, the thickness, the shape at the ends, and the fit. That was the principal adjuster for sound.

The bridge on the violin sits on the top and carries the four strings. The musician draws a long wooden bow across the strings in front of the bridge. This bow, made of a wood called pernambuco, is strung with horse mane or tail that is covered with dried tree resin, called rosin. There are a few options for altering sound with the bridge. These include changing the quality and hardness of the maple used, the age of the wood, the fit of the feet, the size and shape of the cutouts, and the position on the top of the instrument within very small parameters, which is about a millimeter for a violin.

If a violin doesn't sound right, one always checks, or *should* check, the glue joints. The consequences of something not glued properly on a violin include an uncontrollable screaming E string, an extremely ill-tempered musician, lack of harmony in the household of the musician, divorce, economic downturn, and Fruity-O's with FD&C red dye #5 for dinner.

Beyond that, many a violin maker, repairer, and restorer have been truly clueless as to what else to do. They planed a fingerboard because it became rutted and required planing. If the sound changed, and the violin seemed to be better, the maker took the credit for his superior skill and knowledge. If it were judged to be worse, it surely was the persnickety customer having a bad-bow-hair day. The instrument was fine; the client was a few strings short of a fiddle and badly in need of prune juice. Oh, the suffering the poor violin maker had to endure.

One violin-making teacher I had actually told us, "The customer is never your friend." (I had better add here that was not violin-making master Karl Roy, with whom we studied for 16 summers, or Carleen Hutchins with whom we worked for a very long time as well.) Several violin shop owners have confided that they sometimes took the instrument to the back room and only pretended that they had moved the soundpost.

So arose the need to discover more about sound: how to improve on the instruments currently being produced, and how to better adjust the ones already in existence. If someone already had all the answers, I hadn't heard about him or her.

Nearly a decade into my profession as a violin maker, Carleen Hutchins showed me that if she stuck clay on the end of the violin fingerboard, it could substantially change the sound of the instrument.

There is an overall note to the violin that can be heard when you tap with your fingertips on the violin scroll as it is held upside down at the purfling. It is better not to use a big hammer for this. If you read "The Introduction" you may recall that a framing hammer is not considered a violin-making tool. (And if you didn't read "The Introduction," only extreme guilt will expunge this fact from your permanent record.) So, heavy hammers and violins are mutually exclusive, except as it is written in the bylaws where it is a pardonable misdemeanor if used by a parent who can't bear to hear one more outburst from a plywood violin-shaped box with strings.

As clay is added to the end of the fingerboard, the tapping note sounds lower in pitch. The more clay is added, the lower the pitch. Carleen noticed that when she got this tapping to be the same as the note she heard when she was blowing across the *f* holes (s-shaped slots cut into the top), the sound got better. I heard the same thing. Carleen also showed there were positive changes when she tested the instruments with her electronic equipment. She published a paper about her findings in the *Journal of the Catgut Acoustical Society* in 1985. Carleen had founded the Catgut Society in 1963 for the purpose of furthering acoustical research on the bowed string instruments.

As it was not the height of fashion to have clay stuck on someone's instrument, I studied Carleen's paper in order to figure out how to eliminate the clay. I wanted to find ways to make the acoustical changes so that they could be incorporated into the wood of an instrument and be part of the normal set-up.

I found that planing the fingerboard—removing shavings of wood with a hand tool called a plane—also lowered the body note. Shortening the fingerboard raised the body note, which could not be achieved by adding clay anywhere on the instrument. This result appeared to be predictable thanks to earlier work done by physicist Ken Marshall showing how the violin vibrates at different notes. In May of 1987, I published the findings of my research in the *Journal of the Catgut Acoustical Society.*

At that time I did not have access to equipment like Carleen's, and I did not have the equipment I now have. I worked with extremely patient musicians to determine the best sound, and as a result began to match the body note to something somewhat lower in pitch than the one Carleen had been using. However, at the time I published my paper neither Carleen nor I realized this.

I was singing into the instrument through the *f* holes and finding the note at which the entire instrument vibrated. This pitch was noticeably louder, and I easily could feel the wood quivering in my fingers. For most violins this note was about middle C on the piano. The *f* hole blowing pitch was usually closer to a D, the note just above middle C. When I matched the body tap to the whole body vibration note by planing or shortening the fingerboard, whichever was needed, the sound was even better than matching the body tap to the *f* hole blow note, as Carleen had done.

It wasn't until after the publication of my article, when Carleen was testing some instruments I'd "mode matched," that she realized I had learned to match the body tap pitch to something below the *f* hole blow note. I then named this singing vibration "the Zaltone." It was not found with measuring equipment. The Zaltone pitch is best identified by singing into the instrument and moving the frequency of the voice until the vibrating point becomes apparent. These discoveries occupied me for a while and I began to "mode match" everything resembling a violin that came through my hands.

Carleen then suggested that I look into the tuning of the tailpiece. Oh sure, it sounded innocent enough. She probably even meant well. But it was not pretty. Finally, after some months, the tailpieces and I agreed upon a temporary cease-fire. I had multiple wounds to heal and had inflicted a bit of damage of my own to the tailpiece camp. Handmade tailpieces. Very expensive handmade tailpieces. Very expensive handmade tailpieces, which I had bought. Hey, wait a minute! Unbowed, they just laughed at me, knowing that sooner or later I would be back—and on my knees.

I eventually was compelled to return to the research, because, as the tailpieces knew all along, the note at which they vibrate is critical to the sound. Part of the problem was that I had a preconceived notion about what pitch I should be using. Carleen's research, which had achieved success at the tailpiece pitch I was currently trying, was disaster for me when it was used on a violin whose body tap was matched to the Zaltone. (She had done her tailpiece research based on the body tap matched to the *f* hole blow pitch, which was an important step, but we now know is not the very best arrangement.) I kept messing up the sound of the violins and was getting more and more, uh, perplexed. Yes, that's it, perplexed—just a gentle low key spiritual sort of bewilderment that we spiritual types do from time to time so as not to raise our voices, or get red in the face, or find the hammer in order to pulverize those, um, gosh darn little pieces of wood into unrecognizable splinters.

Eventually, every single violin whose tailpiece I had matched to be an octave below the singing tone note (Zaltone), after previously matching the body tap to the singing tone note (Zaltone), sounded like it had just been filled with a hydrogenated-genuine-fake-imitation-propylene-glycol-enriched soup. My dog wouldn't come near me. I felt a slight stirring in the air about me as the gentle tippety tappety of the glue-laminated beams my guides were now taking turns dropping on my oblivious cranium made contact. Oh. *Don't determine what works best until you actually do the research and learn what works best.* Or call the psychic hotline.

At too long last, I found that if the body tap were to be placed at the best note (the Zaltone), then the tailpiece absolutely had to *not* be an octave below that Zaltone note. Furthermore, the most beautiful sound is obtained in the following way. Sing into the fiddle until it vibrates the most (about a C). Then change the note slightly going up with the voice, until you no longer feel the body vibrate (about a D), or down until the body no longer vibrates (about a B or B flat.). An octave below either of these notes will be the correct one for the tailpiece.

Hutchins had found one of the correct notes at approximately the D. That was the f hole blow note. But she had placed the other note on the octave below the Zaltone, which, when body tap is matched to singing tone (Zaltone), has that filled-with-cream-of-emulsified-antifreeze-enriched-soup effect. So for this arrangement one goes a bit lower, until the body does not vibrate to the voice. It seems as if the tailpiece tuned to the octave frequency of the body tap and Zaltone is too much vibration at the same note. Somehow the sound of the fiddle is absorbed or compromised. I highly recommend the other arrangement, which I described. The family dog will appreciate it

The next breakthrough began quite by accident, and took a few more years to figure out. Now that I am writing this, I need no longer gaze into the mirror and wonder where all the years went. Memory has been stored in both hard copy and soft copy—this book and my face.

I was doing some research with physics professor and acoustician George Bissinger. (I shall have to ask him if he wants his last name in this book.) I was trying to stiffen the ribs of a violin by attaching thin pieces of wood to them with double stick tape. George had transported lots of fancy and expensive equipment to our house to help with the experiment. If I had succeeded in stiffening the ribs, I would have been in a position to test a way to make certain violins sound better, based on a hypothesis of Hutchins.

Alas, my attempts to stiffen the ribs in this manner were a dismal failure. We were getting ready, after several days of research, to fold our soggy tents when my student, Gary (who is not sure he wants his last name in this book "if it's going to be too weird"), noticed that when I stuck a piece of wood on a particular rib in a particular spot, the instrument sounded better. We tried it on a couple of other violins, and they sounded better too. George said, "You are adding mass, not stiffness." So I tried adding a bit of clay instead of wood, and got the same results. In fact, at the time, I had a client's $50,000 instrument at our home and workshop and his sounded better with the extra attachment also. My client came to pick up his instrument and agreed with us. So he went home with a small piece of wood stuck to his violin's rib in just the right spot.

George went back to North Carolina, Gary went home, and I spent the next week awake all night, every night, trying to figure out what was going on. This was new ground and there was no one to guide me—at least that I knew about. It was a time of ecstasy and insanity for me. I knew there were important secrets to uncover.

Eventually I found six spots that especially affected the sound when clay was put on one or more of them. This later became 12 spots, all on the ribs. So for a period of time, owners of our instruments, professional musicians all, had pieces of clay or bits of wood stuck to their instrument's ribs. I'm sure this did wonders for our reputation. Unfortunately for my husband, he was judged guilty by association.

We heard a story from one musician that she was on a job and noticed her instrument was being eyed by another musician. The other musician then turned her violin to reveal small pieces of wood fastened to it. They were additional pieces not unlike that of the first musician's instrument. They nodded to each other solemnly and went on playing—no explanation necessary.

I decided that by the same physics principles I had used to do the fingerboard work, if there were a place to add clay to increase the quality of the sound, there should be a place to scrape to get the same effect. Points and counterpoints. More all-nighters. It took me three years to master this new procedure. Various musicians, who could be nominated for sainthood, helped me for hours and hours until we had 100% pure, rolled, formed, pressed, irradiated, reconstituted, genetically "modifried" soy substitute for brains. Violin? Food processor? Barking dog? Who could tell?

To begin the learning process, I volunteered my very first violin, scraping through the varnish on the outside. Since the instrument looked to be worse than a beginner's effort and was kept hidden from public view, I figured that willing its body to science would only increase its value, and add meaning and purpose to its previously sad existence. Then I fashioned scrapers so that I could reach inside the violin—through the *f* holes—and removed very tiny amounts of sawdust, barely perceptible to the eye. The violin sound could be considerably improved if I scraped enough of the right points in the right order, but it took a long time. All the techniques I was developing were used on violins, violas, and cellos, although for the purpose of writing I may use the word "violins" when referring to the entire group.

After I had practiced the rib scraping for some time, George Bissinger came to visit on university break, bringing a carload of acoustical test equipment. Every time George comes he always spends the first two days trying to get the electronics to work right. So far we are about 10 for 10 on this one. He amuses himself by eating Pecan Sandies and I have yet to see him lose his temper.

The obligatory act of computer breakdown and electronic healing completed, we took an instrument I had made early in my career (named UDI for Ugly Duckling) and George began the absolutely agonizingly slow process of modal analysis. The method shows how an instrument is moving at each different frequency, as well as the nodal lines, which are places where the instrument does not move. Each run of tests takes all day and is an unbelievably grueling (and frankly, in my opinion, boring) task to get all the data loaded into the computer where it can be analyzed. George measured UDI first before I did anything, and then measured again, after I spent some hours improving the sound by scraping the inside of the ribs in the appropriate spots.

Gary, whose last name I will take to my grave, or at least hold it until I get to the acknowledgements section, came to help me with the sound adjustment. Having Gary play, enabled me to stand away from the instrument. I made better acoustical judgments from that listening perspective.

After some days of testing, George returned to North Carolina and I heard nothing from him for months. Eventually I got a package. It was the computer analysis of all those days of soporific measurements showing the effects of the rib scraping; those almost imperceptible bits of sawdust removed over hours of brain and ear numbing time showed a big change in the motion of the violin. And furthermore, the nodal lines moved to a position we would have predicted if the sound were going to improve. I was thrilled. This was scientific validation in a big way.

A general description of the method born out of several years of experiments and practice was to place a fingertip on the 12 points of the ribs while I plucked a string. As a finger is placed at various spots, the plucked sound will either seem the same, or slightly higher or brighter, or slightly lower or more "thuddy." Although the actual note was not changing, the overtones, which are vibrations that occur at various frequencies above a note, were changing, depending upon where I placed my finger. A difference in the overtones is what gives variety of sound between instruments. So, for example, an oboe and a trumpet, playing the exact same note, will have a different set of overtones. And two different oboes will have similar but different overtones and will sound somewhat different, at least to an oboist.

If the overtones sounded higher at a particular spot when my finger was placed there, I then substituted a small piece of clay for my finger. The musician played the instrument, I listened, and together we decided if the violin sounded better with the clay in that spot. If we agreed that it was better, it meant that lowering the perceived pitch of the spot that sounded higher helped the vibrations of the violin to bring it closer to overall balance. To make the change permanent, the same effect was achieved by raising the overtones of the counterpoint spot—a spot that always has a low sound to the pluck—if the other spot is high. (There are six separate strips of maple making up the ribs of a violin. The counterpoint spot is in a specific place on the same maple strip.) To raise the overtones of the low counterpoint spot, I reached inside through the *f* hole with my special scraper on a bent rod, and scraped that counterpoint spot, the one with the low sound that corresponds to the high spot I had tested with clay.

The idea is to have all the overtones at each of the 12 spots sound alike. So after scraping one spot until it balanced its partner spot, the musician and I went around again looking for the next spot to fix. And around. And around. And around. When one or both of us couldn't take it anymore or couldn't hear anymore, or both, we discussed the wisdom of taking a break—and kept going. We would have made a great commercial for organic foods: "This is your brain on Polysorbate 80."

The changes in sound from the rib tuning procedure were far from trivial. The rib scraping salvaged the sound of William Steck's Peresson violin (William Steck was the Concertmaster of the National Symphony in Washington, D.C. at the time) after my husband and I found it necessary to reline a rib because it had buckled under the chinrest. All that added material in a very sensitive spot caused a minor panic when we got the instrument back together and noticed that the sound had vanished to parts unknown. No amount of soundpost moving would have restored it, either.

Thank goodness my rib scraping knowledge, although not particularly refined at that point, had arrived just ahead of this repair. Thank goodness Bill trusted me to do this new procedure on his instrument and thank the traffic angels and my violist friend, Bonnie Cohen, who was able to get across The Woodrow Wilson Bridge day after day—a small miracle in itself. Bonnie came to help me adjust Bill's violin so he didn't have to hear what it sounded like until its beautiful tone was restored. I was drowning in enough adrenaline as it was.

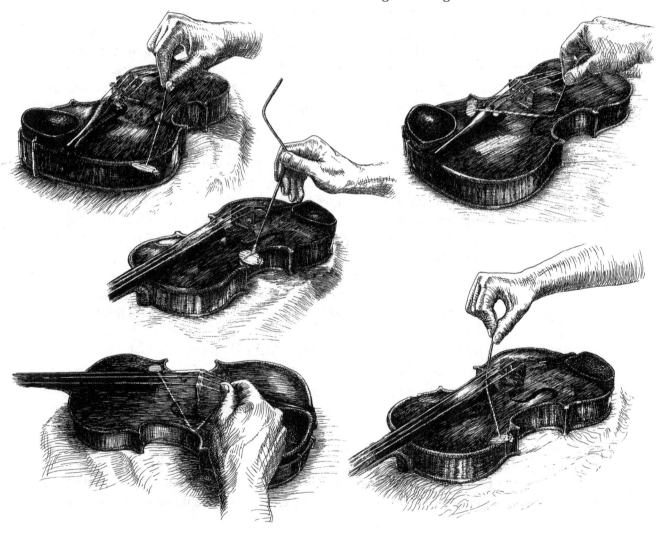

The thing about rib tuning is that it rests on getting the fingerboard tuning and then the tailpiece tuning correct first. This order is absolutely critical. How do I know this? Well . . . the scriptwriters of my life evidently had been watching too many *I Love Lucy* reruns and decided to try their hand at comedy.

My husband had gotten a commission from a violist in the Jacksonville Symphony. We were late with the viola by several months. I say we, because after he finishes the main instrument, he graciously turns it over to me for the set-up and acoustic work. The violist had an upcoming audition and wanted to use her new viola.

I completed the initial set-up, which consisted of making a bridge and a soundpost. I planed the fingerboard and matched the body tap to the Zaltone. I could hear that the viola still needed something. I began to tune the ribs without checking the tailpiece resonance. (Add laugh track here.) I was working by myself without a musician to play, which would have offered me the opportunity to hear the instrument from across the room, although in this case it may not have mattered.

After spending many hours scraping the most minuscule amounts of wood imaginable, things inexplicably seemed to be going in the wrong direction soundwise. The violist called from Florida and inquired as to delivery date. I didn't have an answer, not a good one anyway. I continued to work away diligently. To my amazement things were still going in the wrong direction. Best to rest my ears and try again another day. I don't remember for how long this went on, or what I said to the owner. I do remember that I finally sang into the instrument for some reason and discovered that it had no vibration whatsoever, no matter what pitch I tried. I put the recalcitrant thing down and headed for something chocolate.

I returned to the scene of the crime and made another attempt to awaken the wooden creature with my decidedly non-dulcet and rapidly disintegrating tones. Not surprisingly, although the chocolate offered temporary respite, I had not emerged into another reality, and the viola was just as unresponsive as it had been several hundred calories earlier.

Every violin or viola I have ever sung into has had a Zaltone—a note that causes the instrument to resonate, reflect my voice, and vibrate my fingers. And I have sung into a large, quivering quantity of instruments from those constructed of cheap plywood to priceless Stradivaris. I didn't think it was possible for a violin or viola to be absolutely and completely dead; there was no response anywhere on any note when one sang inside. My dog carefully studied the situation for half a second, packed a snack, and headed for the neighbor's.

I don't know what poor pitiable etheric messenger pigeon drew the short straw and was sent to find its way through the thick, overcooked, murky mush that surrounded my head. Evidently he had taken the course in how to make an instrument-only bad weather landing, as I found myself picking up the viola and tapping the tailpiece. It was exactly on the Zaltone, as was the body tap. The body tap was there because I had planed the fingerboard to the right thickness so it would be there. The tailpiece was there, well, because it was.

I had never checked it. All those years of struggling to learn how to tune the tailpiece, and I had never checked it. "Why was that?" I might have inquired of myself. But just then the bell rang. I grabbed my books and headed for the door—maybe it was the end of the school day. I was hopeful. Oh it was Ma Bell. I picked up the phone. It was the violist in Florida.

Having the tailpiece at the worst possible frequency (which probably kept it from sounding as it could have right from the start) had caused me to make exactly backwards decisions about where to scrape the ribs. Every time the fiddle would have sounded better, the tailpiece absorbed the sound, leaving me to think the right spots were the wrong ones, and vice versa. I elevated the art of "mis-scraping" to such a degree that I had created an object worthy of being a flowerpot shaped like a violin. I don't think I could have done that if I had tried. I don't think I could do it again.

That flowerpot image came to me for two reasons; Bob and I often saw a magazine advertisement: *What's He Doing? He's Creating a Concrete Flower Pot . . . And You Can, Too!* It became a family joke. I couldn't help but think that as I held this very expensive assemblage of wooden parts (carefully and lovingly constructed by my husband over a period of many months), which somehow had stopped vibrating, that *Yes, I Could and I Had, Too!*

The second reason for this image was because of an experience my husband had before we met. He had undertaken a repair on a violin and labored away mightily to achieve a good sound. Because the customer was a colleague, Bob decided to do all the work without charge. Bob finally completed the repairs and adjustments, the man picked up his fiddle, thanked Bob, and left. My husband heard nothing for weeks. Eventually, when Bob happened to see the gentleman again, he could not contain his curiosity and asked his colleague how he liked the repaired instrument. "It looks fine," the man replied. "Yes," said Bob, "but how does it sound?" "Sound?" the man asked with a totally blank look. "I put dirt in it, planted it with ivy, and put it on the mantel." Bob doesn't do repairs anymore.

Now, years later, I held in my hands an instrument that, while not as water-worthy as a flowerpot, probably sounded very similar to one. I fired my scriptwriters and got a couple of new ones from a temp service. I specifically requested those who had no access to television, except PBS. I put a different tailpiece on our Florida-bound viola, and got it tuned to the correct frequency. Even now, doing this perfectly is a bit tricky. I then proceeded to start the rib tuning all over again. I don't remember how long this took; I was measuring time by the number of bags of potato chips that I consumed. Eventually, the viola's resonance came back. A beautiful sound issued forth from the instrument—once I got a musician there to play it. I could no longer fit into my clothes.

We met the new owner the next day, in the parking lot of a hotel in South Carolina. As she played, a cat came up to us making overtures to everyone. We have photos. When a cat approves, you know you've nailed it. On second thought, perhaps nailed is not quite the right image.

Living Life—One Bag of Chips at a Time

Listening to the tailpiece

You know it's time for a rest when you hear: The area code you seeketh hath been changed. The number you dialeth is not in service. If you wisheth assistance, all our customer representatives doth currently toil. If you useth a touchtone, presseth whatever. Your wait time is approximately fourscore and ten. We beseech thee: Have a nice day. Click.

CHAPTER II

Age Before Beauty

Doctors go through a tremendous amount of training and testing in order to be licensed. Many of them are real healers, but at least a few lack sufficient skill or personal integrity despite a long education.

In this country, unlike Germany, there are no requirements for the training of violin makers. There is no certification or license involved. Any Tom, Darren, or Harriet can pick up a hammer and hang out a shingle that says "expert master." And plenty of them do, some of them seemingly doing their repair work with that very same hammer.

Too many somewhat less than "expert masters" have ruined priceless instruments. Over the centuries the violin-making profession has been rife with its share of fraud, such as label switching or fake identification papers. There's money to be made. It can give individuals who are trustworthy and competent or even true masters of the craft an unfortunate and undeserved reputation.

Some challenged humans may tarnish the image of their profession, but most people agree that at least some doctors do heal and some violin makers repair, restore, and make new instruments well (or well enough). I think there is also the assumption that many in both groups are honest and no more deluded than anyone else.

Then we come to intuitives. I've seen countless TV shows that purport to expose fraudulent or supposedly fraudulent psychics one after the other and conclude that all intuitives are either con artists or at least flaky. If a few quacks reflect badly on all ducks, then we shouldn't trust any doctors, or violin makers, or lawyers for that matter—and there go a lot of good jokes.

Acceptance that there is such a thing as a genuine intuitive (telepath, psychic, channel, clairvoyant or medium) with extra-sensory abilities is spreading. However, we are far from a place where someone can write the sort of book you are now reading and expect to be invited to universities for honorary Ph.D.s. I don't think I will be applying for NSF grants either. I don't even want to tell the company that processes the credit card numbers I accept that I am other than "violin maker."

One friend, an extraordinary medium who also happens to have a Ph.D., was dropped by the company that allowed her to accept credit card payments when they found out what she did for a living. Perhaps only the IRS doesn't care, just so you report your income. And I'm not too sure about that either. I'm still filing as a violin maker and acoustician. Oops. Well, they wouldn't be reading this book anyway.

As I mentioned in "The Introduction," it has been my great fortune to journey into the arena of metaphysics with the best. If a person demonstrates that they have received specific information that could not have been learned through the usual physical senses, wild guessing or clever knowledge of psychology, it bears more than serious consideration.

Unfortunately, many people are frightened by the idea that reality could be ordered in any way other than the one they perceive or that scientists say is real because they have measured it with equipment. The scope of what exists as far as the general public is concerned is increasing daily because scientific equipment is improving. However, things do not exist only as they are discovered by pieces of hardware. Those people who claim to see, feel or otherwise perceive energy fields, thoughts, or etheric beings, until the equipment to measure them catches up are likely to be considered a few notes short of a symphony. For many people, the extra senses of humans are not to be trusted—ever. If they allow one piece of intuitive stuff to be true, they have to rethink their entire world. What with jobs, taxes, kids, meals, laundry, mechanical breakdowns, bills, and facial hair, who has time for deep philosophical reflection?

Some of us have felt compelled to make the time, perhaps at the expense of a few of those things on the above list, or, as an alternative: sleep. For many of this group the journey into the expansion of our abilities has been a wonderful, awe-inspiring adventure. For another segment of the population, the whole idea of the existence of multi-dimensional energy fields and disembodied consciousness is far too scary to even contemplate. Some would just as soon find reasons to discount the evidence and make unflattering judgments about intuitive practitioners or those who believe these skills exist.

As a healer, it is not my job to convince anyone. It is my job to help those who are open enough, and in some cases desperate enough, to want to try. Often it is desperation and struggle that leads us to good places we otherwise would never have gone. I assume there is a gentler way to evolve, but that course doesn't seem to be offered this semester.

I tried to be mercifully brief in my little attempt to remind those skeptical readers (who I commend for even getting this far) that perhaps there is reason to consider the possibility of individuals whose psychic gifts are genuine, never mind what they have seen on TV. My next leap into new knowledge of how to use physical means to further the art of acoustical adjustment on the violin came from these unusual sources, not the fakes and the flakes, but the real clairvoyants and clairaudients. The solid, well-grounded ones, whose accuracy can be quite impressive.

Because of the nature of free will, which creates a new future in each moment, I don't recommend using intuitives for prediction, but rather as a source of information. For example, a gifted medical intuitive or general all-purpose clairvoyant can look at a person's energy field to determine what physical, emotional, or mental changes would be advised in order to avoid or heal an illness. Judging from personal experience, I would say that our weatherpersons and all their scientific equipment would be lucky to be so reliable. Genuine intuitives do indeed exist beyond the fantasies of Star Trek. And frankly, if someone thought I were totally hopeless as a violin maker, I sure wouldn't be volunteering to be on their television show to demonstrate my dexterity with a soundpost setter. I'd probably find a way to drop it inside the fiddle.

My next leap of wisdom was preceded by struggle—for a change. Although I still aspire to progress without the inspiration of agony, sometimes the frustrations and failures that always seem to come before personal growth and new knowledge are hilarious in hindsight, which fact gives rise to the classic definition of humor as "tragedy plus time." When I finished writing the first draft of the previous chapter, I read it to my mother over the phone. After listening to me recount the tale of the viola rendered nearly soundless, she inquired with shock, "That was Bob's viola?" Yes, it *was*. Indeed it was temporarily ruined, and I managed to do all that by removing immeasurably small amounts of wood over many hours of time. Such is my talent. Why do anything easily and gracefully when it can be done otherwise?

Because my husband has taken "struggle" and honed it to a fine art, I failed to resist including a sample of a "Bob day" in this chapter. His journals offer clarification of why we humans need eternity to "get it." Unless of course we already have been through all eternity and earth is the place where those of us who are still lagging have been placed.

I know all that spiritual stuff about being in the moment, but frankly sometimes I'd rather look back at the moment from a safe distance. Maybe spiritual evolution is to be able to laugh *in* the moment, but there is only so much soul advancement one can stand when in the middle of building a house or a violin.

I'm hoping that a sense of humor after the fact at least affords us some little gold sticky stars on our life lesson books if only we can remember to bring those books to class in the first place. I would bring mine if I could remember the location of my locker. I've had countless dreams wandering around some school looking for it. At least in my most recent dreams I'm fully clothed. I'm hoping that's a sign of progress.

I include here a few pages from my husband's journal, as he builds the Frank Lloyd Wright Prairie-style house and healing center he designed for us in Ithaca, New York. At the same time and right next to our house, he built our friend Alex's house (also a Prairie-style design). Here was April 11, 1999 from Robert J. Spear's perspective.

April 11, 1999 Sunday

A Greek tragedy kind of day, Bob style, and a weak end to the weekend. After wallowing in sloth for the past two days, I decided it was time to take myself in hand and apply some effort toward finishing the job at Alex's house—in particular the installation of the "skinny-mini" stacked clothes washer and dryer we got from Debra. This focus was not only the result of a harsh scrutiny of priorities, but also of a dearth of clean underwear in the Spear studio. I'd be damned if I were going to spend any more cash on underwear when my duffel bag is absolutely stuffed full of garments that I had worn only once. At some point, all those clothes had to be washed, and today was the day I planned to do that come hell or high wa—oops, shouldn't have said that.

After munching a breakfast suitable in size to give me more than enough energy for the day's tasks, I returned to the site and donned my work duds before playing a few hands of Free Cell on the computer. That chore behind me, I decided to peel off an hour and use it to begin cleaning up my room in preparation for a visit from my Sweetie in less than two weeks. I have been storing all the paints, caulks, glue, sealers, and stains inside the studio over the winter to keep them from freezing, but they have made my room look like a warehouse that's even more impossible to clean than it usually is. I fired up my DR Power Wagon, which, to my amazement, started on the first pull. Then I loaded up all the stored materials until the entire wagon was filled. Then I conveyed the cargo over to the confines of the basement in the big house. Then a thunderstorm passed over, then the temperature dropped, and then it started to snow! Really, I wouldn't lie to you about this.

Wickes had delivered about ten three-packs of Miraflex for Alex's under-floor insulation, but they had stacked it neatly outside the front door of the wrong house, so I DR'ed it to the Thornhill cottage and stacked it just inside the garage door. Then I fired up the pump and was delighted to observe that the water was running clear, so there was no more excuse for delay. The time had come to wet cloth, to suds duds, to slosh shirts, to rinse pants, to tumble towels, to—well, you get the idea!

I moved the mini from the garage to Alex's basement using the hand truck, bumping and bouncing across the terrain, the mini, the truck, and I looking like a flock of geese flying in loose formation. After pausing mid-field to repair a flat tire, I grunted the machine through the basement door and moved it into location. Ah, perfection! Barely an inch to spare on either side between the drain and hose fittings on the left and the 220-volt electrical receptacle on the right. It even looked as though we had done it that way on purpose.

Then I had to replace the mini's outmoded three-prong plug with a modern four-prong plug, which meant going inside the back of the dryer to make the modification. I love American mechanical design which puts the screws for the wire ends just far enough inside the compartment so that a) they can't be reached, and b) the knife-like edges of the steel compartment cut your hands to ribbons as you try. I also admire how American bean-counters have shaved the costs of production by using the shortest length of screw possible consistent with frustration. There is about a quarter-turn difference between having the screw backed out far enough to allow the wire to fit underneath, and far enough to cause the screw to fall out of the hole.

Now when the latter occurs, the screw goes one of two places. Either it lands inside the compartment and rolls under the wiring harness so that all the wires that were just connected have to be disconnected, or it falls to the floor. Now when the latter occurs, one expects to search around for the screw for a while since an escaped screw takes freedom very seriously and does not want to be returned to its compartment to get screwed again. But, remember, we are not dealing simply with a dropped screw here, but with a Bob-dropped screw, which is something else all together. In front of my weak, horrified eyes, the screw hit the floor, bounced up toward the drywall, passed between the edge of the drywall and the next stud, which was an opening about three-quarters of an inch wide, hit the floor again, bounced up again, and flew against a piece of scrap lumber that just happened to be lying on the floor at the precise angle needed to make the screw bounce off the scrap and hit the side of a piece of pex tubing coming out of the radiant floor manifold. The screw then slid down the inside curve of the pex tube until it passed between the tube and the pvc sleeve that protects the tube from the concrete, and disappeared down the sleeve and under the floor. Really, I wouldn't lie to you about this!

Tell me, someone, I said aloud, how many years would I have to sit here and how many millions of screws would I have to throw on the floor toward the drywall before one followed the same path and slid between the pex tube and the pvc sleeve—a space barely larger than the screw itself—and vanished beneath the concrete floor? Five years? Ten? Twenty? About the same time it would take for a chimpanzee sitting in front of a piano to master the instrument, rule lines by hand on a ream of score paper, and set down Beethoven's Seventh Symphony?

After a lengthy search, I found one screw out of the thousands on the site that would fit the wiring bus. I taped it to the screwdriver blade and I rejoiced in the sight of my shredded hands because if they were bleeding it meant that my hands, and presumably the screws, were still inside the wiring compartment. After a few more advances and retreats, it was time to pop off the protective plate on the washer standpipe and insert the discharge hose.

Pat, the plumber, had instructed me to pry off the plug since, he swore, it was just tacked in place with a few drops of glue. After trying to slip a thin blade between the plug and the plastic and meeting with no success whatsoever, I switched to progressively larger screwdrivers until I ended up bashing on the plug with a large-bladed screwdriver driven by blows from my big

Vaughn framing hammer. No, this little pluggie was not about to pop off. I stormed my brain and decided that I would outwit myself and take a more surgical approach. I would make an incision in the middle of the plug into which I would insert my little pry bar and use the power of the lever to make that recalcitrant closure yield.

I finally succeeded in making the incision, and began applying force to the end of the pry bar, smirking the entire time. At last, I tore the plug free. Unfortunately, as it popped off the drain pipe it split into two unequal parts. The little part fell on the floor and lay there like a piece of white bread with the peanut-butter side down. The other, larger, part flew up and hit the side of the recessed drain fixture bounced out and hit me in the chest, bounced back inside the recessed compartment, bounced against the valve handle of one of the supply lines, which handle was at precisely the right angle to deflect the errant piece into the center of the fixture where, right in front of my weak and horrified eyes, it vanished down the drain. It fell into the opening without even touching the sides! A piece, mind you, that is only a bit smaller in diameter than the drain pipe itself. No, really, I wouldn't lie to you about this.

Tell me, I inquired of the deity, how many years would I have to sit here and how many millions of broken plastic scraps would I have to throw against my chest before one followed the same path and slid down the drain pipe and lodged in the trap of the washing machine I was just about to use for the first time? Five years? Ten? Twenty? About the same time it would take for a dolphin sitting in front of a computer to figure out how to turn the machine on, master the C programming language and write the Windows 2000 operating system?

Clearly, the gods were displeased with my efforts, but I was determined to press on. Battered, bleeding but unbowed, I installed the dryer vent, connected the supply hoses, wired a 30-amp breaker in the main panel, connected the pressure switch, threw on all the breakers, and stood there smirking until absolutely nothing happened. The pressure switch had foiled me again.

Tonight I went to K-Mart and bought another week's worth of underwear.

The house is beautiful. The instruments, sooner or later, or even later in our case, turn out beautifully too—usually. It is the getting from here to there that for many of us has little connection to grace.

Singing Woods

CHAPTER III

Bar-Ode Time

It was a viola. Again. We had heard it said by a well-known *former* violin maker that when you are dealing with violists, you are dealing with desperate people. In that moment, the same could be said for the viola maker. I needed to do something for this viola—poor thing, it had just been born and already its Godmother was displeased.

The viola had an owner. Worse, it was mostly paid for. Even worse, the money had already been spent. I thought it unwise to count on months of "playing in" to bring out those soul-stirring sounds. Handing the owner her new viola complete with a complimentary box of earplugs did not seem to be a wise career move.

The tailpiece was not the difficulty this time. Nor were the ribs. I was out of ideas, but I had no other job skills—I'd been a luthier too long. What was the problem with this instrument? Was it actually just fine but I had grown ridiculously fussy? Or was it really a candidate for begonias? I decided it was the latter.

The only explanation for this acoustical calamity was those scriptwriters again. I thought things had been rolling along acceptably. Whatever temps had taken over the job of writing the text of my life since the firing of the *I Love Lucy* junkies, had appeared to be, if not inspired, at least good enough. Now I realized that I was starring in a cooking show. The oven was at 450 degrees Fahrenheit and heating slowly. I was dinner.

I looked at the viola. It was mercifully silent for the moment. What choices remained? The only thing I could think of was to take my chances with yet another set of writers. This exchange accomplished, it was clear I now had the unemployed crew from the old *Twilight*

Zone TV series. How could I tell? It wasn't difficult. With not a glimmer of a watt in my head as to how to remedy the musically dysfunctional viola, I decided I could try asking a guide—those guys I couldn't see. I figured they had to be there as we humans were far too clueless to be left entirely on our own down here. Now I knew I wasn't clearly hearing my guidance. I thought history had demonstrated that. However, I had had enough positive experience with mediums to trust in the existence of invisible guides, and humans who could receive their thoughts accurately enough to be of use.

The telepaths are like people who see color in a world where "normal" people see only black and white (and think that is all there is), or who hear in a world where "normal" people are deaf (and believe only in silence). When those with extra senses try to explain to "normal" people about the existence of color and sound they are sometimes considered two players short of a duet, or turned into material for science fiction entertainment. Still, it beats the old routine of burning at the stake.

During the years described in Chapter I, when I was learning fingerboard, rib, and tailpiece tuning work, I didn't know anyone who was a clear enough telepathic conduit to possibly be able to obtain the kind of very specific information I hoped for. And I didn't know if this sort of thing had even been done in violin acoustics. I rather doubted it.

In the past, violin makers had appeared to be a stuffy bunch, either not big on innovation, or secretive, or both, and not real thrilled with women violin makers, either. I don't think there were any lady luthiers until recently.

Some years before, I did have some sessions with intuitive Fred Mansbridge, who was still alive (in physical form) at that time. He gave me some important clues that I didn't heed until years later. It had something to do with touching the wood with love. At the time it sounded to me like a lot of fluff. *Live and don't learn.*

I have since come to recognize that I had been getting assistance as I was learning the rib tuning procedures. I was totally unaware of it as guidance at the time, but at least I paid attention at some level of consciousness since I got the information. I think we are often helped, but don't recognize it.

By the time I was out of culturally acceptable ideas as to what to do with this particular viola, I had made more than the acquaintance of Marlene Sandler. Every now and again I saw a little blurb on TV about people who had the gift of communicating with animals. Some of the shows were actually open-minded about people who had telepathic abilities and could pick up the thoughts of the animals in whatever way these occurred, such as pictures, words, feelings, or in a manner we cannot describe. Our dog, Poco, was starting to have various problems and I wanted to be able to communicate with him in more specific ways. But I couldn't seem to ever find one of these "animal communicators."

Eventually, I was given a videotape by my friend Jill King about "Tellington Touch," a specific way of touching your animal companion, which had been shown to create changes in brain wave patterns. It could help create calm and better health in animals. I called the phone number on the video. The lady who answered the phone gave me the number of a local practitioner. I called her. She listened to my story and said, "You need an animal communicator." Yes! Where do I find one?!!!! She gave me several names but suggested Marlene Sandler was the best one for me to try first. Marlene, trained as a counselor, had recently added animal communication to her professional practice. I wasted no time in calling her.

When I first contacted Marlene, I did not have violins in mind. I was seeking communication and help for my dog. The sessions with her were eye-opening. Most were carried out long distance—over the phone—because telepathy, like energy healing, exists in dimensions that are not affected by physical distance.

Even our electrical engineer friend, Alex, came to believe in animal communication after Poco, through Marlene's communication abilities, recounted an incident to us that only Poco and Alex knew about. Poco tattled on Alex for accidentally stepping on his foot when Alex was taking care of him and we were out of town. Alex was rather startled to hear that his misstep had been revealed. He has no interest whatsoever in psychics or anything else metaphysical. Alex is a man of wires and electrical signals. If it is proven to work, then he's fine with it.

I had always suspected that there was far more to the mental and emotional world of animals than just wanting another snack, although my dog considers my ability to understand his immediate and urgent need for yet another biscuit to be critical. However, this sort of communication does not require telepathy, nor does it usually represent a challenge to any self-respecting dog who has even the dullest wit of a human. (Our dog simply sharpens his nose and pokes my leg until he gets the desired result.) We humans with our superiority complex and unyielding belief that the mind is the brain (and vice versa) are missing more than we are getting. Telepathy is the real mode of communication. Speech is a poor substitute, but it will have to do until all of us expand enough to allow ourselves to be more than we currently are.

Having experienced the clarity of Marlene's channel as far as animal communication, I had nothing to lose by trying some violin making questions—except perhaps a few BTUs from a burning viola. As timing would have it, I happened to have an appointment with full trance medium, Carla Gordan, before I spoke next with Marlene.

Appointments with Carla were few and far between and of a somewhat different nature from those with Marlene. Carla worked in a trance state, not consciously present, and did not remember afterward what had been spoken. This was more similar to the way Seth and his material came through Jane Roberts. The consciousness coming through Carla called herself Mary (not the famous one as far as I know). I had come to know Carla and Marlene within a few weeks of each other. This was after about two decades of being almost completely focused on violins, and not much on the metaphysical.

I learned of Carla from a couple of violists who had purchased our instruments. I waited a year before I called her. When I finally did, the appointment was wonderful. After the initial telephone rendezvous, we met in person and had several more sessions together before the time of the latest viola crisis. It had not occurred to me to ask her about instruments before, but this time I tossed in a question asking what was wrong with the viola and what could I do to help it. She proceeded to describe the bass bar without actually naming it. She called it "the balancer." The bass bar is a long piece of wood made of spruce, which traverses most of the length of the top and is glued inside the violin on the bass side of the spruce top. The way it is carved and shaped is critical to the sound of the violin, viola, and cello. I asked if she meant the bass bar and she said yes. I didn't go beyond that, as there were other questions on other topics and the appointment was just a half an hour.

Shortly afterward, I had an appointment with Marlene. I asked her if she were game to try getting information on violins. She was. As I have come to know Marlene over the years, she has always been more than ready to try something new. Marlene knew absolutely nothing about violins. Holding our session over the phone, we asked for the appropriate guides and waited to see what would happen.

The first thing that happened was a lot of Italian in Marlene's head. "This won't work," she explained to the guide level, "You will have to find a way to translate. I can't understand that." Shortly after that she heard in English: "Why do you have this fool for a channel??!!!"

We soon learned that we had gotten none other than Guarneri del Gesu (Guarneri for short). He and Antonio Stradivari are considered to be the two greatest violin makers that have ever lived. I told him that she was the best channel I had for this sort of information, so if he were willing to help, Marlene was it. He couldn't see how enough information could possibly come through her since she didn't know an *f* hole from a soundpost. We explained that perhaps this situation was more fortunate than it looked. No knowledge of violins or violin making meant she could not color or prejudice the material since she was totally ignorant on the topic. Guarneri was far from convinced, but agreed to proceed.

Shortly thereafter, we were honored by the arrival of Antonio Stradivari and J.B. Vuillaume, the latter a wonderful French maker from the 1800s who had reworked the early violins (including the Stradivaris and Guarneris) to modern measurements. Marlene still has trouble pronouncing Vuillaume's name. It often comes out more like Vrooom, which does not appear to amuse him. Overall though, he comes across as a rather gentle soul and much more low key than our "old Italians." Still later we were joined by Sergio Peresson, whom I had known and worked with when he was alive, and an African drummer whose name Marlene couldn't say, so it became shortened to KU.

I realize that all this sounds quite fantastic. However, the quality of the material and instruction that has come through over the years, and which has worked beyond my wildest dreams, could not (or should not) be denied, regardless of whether one believes in the identities of the colorful set of beings who have blessed us with their presence since that session.

Guarneri was and is the most passionate in transmission and has come across with many a flying and funny insult. Marlene has also found herself subjected to what sounded like quite a bit of Italian swearing, not necessarily directed at her. At one point she repeated some of it to an Italian-speaking friend, who gave her a shocked look and told her to never again say those words in polite company. This was one lively bunch.

Once we were through with the insult section of our first meeting with Guarneri, he grudgingly agreed to see what we could do with our "fool for a channel." I asked about the acoustically challenged viola and what was needed to bring in real beauty of sound. Just as in the session with Carla, I was given a description of the bass bar and Marlene was shown pictures in her mind. Somehow we muddled through and over a series of sessions, a description of how to tune the bar in subtle, but effective ways, while leaving the instrument intact, was given. This feisty group were superb teachers. They gave me enough instruction to begin the new process. They also gave clues without revealing everything, so that I had the opportunity to make discoveries on my own as well.

Eventually, even Guarneri came to appreciate Marlene and to see the wisdom in having a channel who was blissfully ignorant of the topic at hand. Thank goodness Marlene had and has a terrific sense of humor and is willing to be quite irreverent herself. When that happens, Marlene is given a sharp ping at the back of her head. Sometimes the group is not in agreement with each other on a particular point. Occasionally they yell and curse and insult each other. It is all in good fun—I learned later.

It is usually Stradivari and Guarneri who make the biggest ruckus, but with everyone communicating at once, Marlene has to ask the entire herd to kindly back out of her head so she can hear them one at a time. This usually earns her a ping. Apparently as these beings get closer to the earth plane to make connection, they take up more of their earth plane personalities. This boisterous bunch can create a hurting head for Marlene on a particularly argumentative and passionate day. Furthermore, Guarneri has stated on several occasions that in a case of disagreements, I should ignore the others and listen to him as we are the closest. (It's a past life thing.) Marlene soon learned that smelling, feeling, and eating grapefruit after one of these sessions helped a lot. A really charged day came to be known as a "three grapefruit day."

We were launched. After a couple of sessions I decided I wanted to tape record. I didn't bother to ask our rowdy gathering of disembodied spirits what they thought about it. I just plugged in the tape and hooked the recorder to the phone. The breaker tripped. I tried it again. The breaker tripped. Again. Trip. So I asked Marlene if perhaps we should inquire about taping. She asked. "Not yet," was the answer. Now I had done plenty of taping and the breaker had never tripped from that machine or from anything else on that circuit. Nor has it ever tripped since. It was not on a ground fault or fussy breaker.

Ultimately, some time later, I was told I could tape. These early sessions all had to be recorded by hand. At times I couldn't catch all the comments as they went flying by and not always in English. Marlene, always conscious, repeated what she heard, and described what she saw.

Now confirmed independently by two different intuitives, Carla and Marlene, the next step was the bass bar. It became apparent that the bass bar could not have been done in this manner before mastering the rib tuning (the development of which I sweated over for three years) and the tailpiece tuning, which had to be done correctly before the rib tuning was performed. This fact shall never be forgotten, as there is a viola in the Jacksonville Symphony that will serve as a reminder as the wrinkles of linear time practice logarithmic expansion across my countenance.

The bass bar tuning, like the rib tuning, is done on the completed, set-up instrument. I had to design tools that could be used to reach in through the *f* holes and make a very slight subtle scrape in exactly the correct spot on the bass bar. This procedure was then repeated until the bar was "tuned." These tools turned out to be quicker and easier to make than the rib scrapers. Although I needed several of varying shapes for each type of instrument (violin, viola, and cello), they were each made by bending a brass rod and sharpening one end to serve as the scraper. This took me just a few minutes, and indeed my kinked and inelegant tools look like they were made in quite a hurry. My excuse is that I was anxious to learn the bar tuning process itself and was focused on function, not form.

Because the bass bar is made out of spruce, a soft wood, this brass rod arrangement sufficed. The ribs, however, are made of maple, a hardwood. The tools required for wood removal in that situation have actual oval scrapers that I made from hard scraper steel. Each oval scraper was then set into a notch on a bent brass rod and soldered in place.

Unfortunately, my soldering ability is on a par with my violin playing and my cooking. The "Heathkit" radio I built in the ninth grade worked exactly one-half hour before the solder joints self-destructed. I thought it more self-serving to conscript our electrical engineer friend, Alex, for the task of soldering the rib tools since he can solder in his sleep. He obliged and the tools remain in one piece to this day.

Once the scrapers were invented and fashioned, I was ready to reach inside and scrape the appropriate bass bar spots, just as soon as I knew where they were. Between clues from the guides and practicing with the tools on my own, the method for "tuning the bar" became clear. Marlene was shown a picture in her head of holding the violin with the left ear next to the chinrest. The second to the lowest string was plucked contin- uously with the right thumb as a left hand finger was moved along the top, following the area where the bass bar was glued underneath. As the finger was moved along, just as with the ribs, the overtones one heard from the plucked string became brighter and duller at different spots. Just as with the ribs, a finished "tuned" bar had equally bright sound- ing spots everywhere and no dull ones.

Holding the ear near the chinrest, as instructed, helped immensely in picking up these subtleties in the over- tone changes while I was learning to hear more precisely. Unfortunately, it also overloaded my ears more quickly, so I had to be careful not to do this too much—I wasn't, of course.

Another way to check the spots was to simply tap along the top, above the bass bar as before, and listen to the changes in the sound of the taps. The same spots that sounded higher or brighter with the finger on a particular spot while the string was plucked, also had a higher, brighter sounding tap pitch when I used my fingernail to tap directly on the wood in the same spot. The lower, duller plucked string spots had lower, duller tap pitches.

I listened carefully to determine the brightest and the dullest spots. They were supposed to be on the same side of the bridge. I then located the same spot on the bar itself by reach- ing inside the instrument (through the *f* holes) and tapping along the bar with the tool, lis- tening for the dullest tap. I double-checked by plucking the second to the lowest string while touching different spots on the bar with the tool. Once the spot was located, I made a very light swipe with the sharpened end of the brass rod tool. I checked and if all had been done correctly, that spot no longer tapped or plucked dull.

I was told by the guides to draw an imaginary line between the brightest and dullest spot and to pay attention to what happened as I scraped. I found that the brightest and dullest spot moved closer and closer together with each scrape, and eventually converged. Thus, all the spots would then tap or pluck alike (and more to the bright sound), for the section just fin- ished. I was often taught in this manner. I would be told to do something and discover the result for myself. It was also a lesson in how to teach.

There was a difference between the method of scraping the ribs and scraping the bar. With the ribs, one keeps going until the ribs give plucks that sound alike for all 12 finger positions. Performed correctly, the sound of the played instrument keeps getting better and better with each scrape.

With the bass bar scraping, the sound improves for a while and then suddenly gets worse. The secret is that one must go back to the ribs, as soon as this happens, and retune. Now there will be bright and dull spots again on the ribs, even though they had been perfectly tuned before the bar work. Usually there isn't much to do and the sound becomes the best yet as soon as the ribs are reworked.

Anyone trying to tune the bar by this method *before* mastering the rib tuning, is going to be crabby. In fact, all the tuning of the various parts of the violin from the bass bar onward rests on mastery of the rib tuning procedures, which, in my experience, can take a few years. I personally have never heard of anything even remotely resembling the rib tuning I described earlier, and that rests on knowing the tailpiece tuning. So everything else that followed had to wait to be learned.

Eventually, countless carbohydrates later, all the spots along the bass bar of our little viola sounded alike, and fairly bright, and all the rib spots were equal and bright as well. When this has been achieved on a violin, viola, or cello, the instrument is usually noticeably improved and sometimes transformed.

In the case of our viola, it was fortunately the latter. So Sleeping Beauty was kissed by Prince Charming, who in this case was a bent brass rod. She awakened with a song and was whisked off to the castle where she lived happily ever after. The Fairy Godmother ordered larger clothes and went out for ice cream.

CHAPTER IV

Not Just Another Day at the Office

A good bit of the time that Marlene was channeling, she had no idea what she was talking about. Sometimes she would make a mistake, and this was not ignored. Once she inadvertently said "f hole" instead of "bass bar." This earned her a ping in the back of her head. More grapefruit needed at the end of the session.

Sometimes the information came as an answer to my questions. Sometimes the information just came. At one point, when all the bass bar information was, I thought, finished, my lively crew said that there was a fourth frequency, not yet discussed—or even known at all to us earthlings. That was intriguing. What were they up to now? I realized that for the first three frequencies they meant: 1) The singing tone (Zaltone); 2) The overall body tap frequency—called B0 in violin acoustics papers, meaning it is the fundamental wood, or body tone; and 3) The f hole blowing note—called A0 in acoustics journals, meaning it is the fundamental air cavity note (also known as the Helmholz resonance). I voiced my understanding of this, and the mystery of the fourth frequency was then revealed.

Marlene was shown a picture of Antonio Stradivari holding a violin upside down (with the back to the ceiling) while he blew gentle puffs of air across the *f* holes. Then, with the violin still upside down, he tapped with fingertips along the midline of the back and compared the tap note to the upside-down blow note. I actually figured out on my own that blowing in the upside-down fiddle, as Stradivari had shown Marlene, somehow combined the A0 (the *f* hole blow note normally heard right side up) and the Zaltone (the singing tone). I got a "bravissimo" for my insight.

I've been insulted enough by this group that I take the bravissimos gladly when they come. For example, at one point I was told that my bass bar tuning was one step above primitive. Later, when I asked if I had moved up to two steps above primitive, I was curtly reminded to keep my ego out of it—they'd tell me about my progress.

If the upside-down blow note and the back tapping note were not in harmony (the same note), an adjustment would further improve the sound of the fiddle. We were shown that the way to adjust this was a spot on the bass bar. To find this spot I was to tap along the bass side of the back, with my ear near the center bout on the bass side, and listen for the brightest tap. From this spot I was to draw an imaginary parallel line down to the bass bar, where I would find a subtly dull-sounding spot that I was to scrape.

The first time I tried this, Marlene and I were on the phone. She had just received these instructions from the old Italians concerning the unheard of fourth frequency. (She was thrilled that they were in agreement and there was no yelling.) I was in the process of making acoustic adjustments to a viola made by Tom King, one of my violin-making students. I played the viola, and Marlene and I (and whoever else I couldn't see) listened. I held the viola upside down, blowing gentle puffs of air across the *f* holes. I tapped the back. The pitches did not match. I found a tap spot along the back that sounded more resonant and mentally drew a line down to a spot on the bar. It was indeed a slightly duller sound as the violin masters had said.

I reached inside the viola with my bass bar tool and gave the spot a very light scrape. I rechecked the upside-down blow note against the back taps and they now matched. Amazing! I picked up a bow and played. Marlene and I both heard a dramatic change in sound—even with my lack of talent. Marlene exclaimed, "This is not another day at the office!" This tuning process was named "Ears of the Angels" by the violin masters.

As time sped on, Marlene and I continued the acoustics lessons from the spirit guides, whom I have come to think of as "The Feisty Five." How Marlene was able to get the information clearly enough, I don't know, but she did. At one point I faxed her a diagram of the violin and there was much exclaiming, "Oh that's what those are!" We tried a couple of sessions as Marlene looked at the drawings with the parts of the violin clearly labeled. It wasn't long before she concluded that it was easier for her to know nothing. She filed the drawings away and we went back to working, as we had been—with Marlene clueless.

Once the bar was finished, I was ready for the next process. This turned out to be ƒ hole tuning. I know of another maker who adjusts sound using small changes to the ƒ holes; however, the method I learned from the masters is quite different, requires knowledge of the rib tuning, and results in much greater transformations to the sound. During the process of ƒ hole tuning, as in bass bar tuning, after a certain number of points are scraped, the sound of the instrument suddenly gets worse rather than better. That means that it is time to go back to the ribs and retune them.

The ƒ hole points are discovered by placing a finger around the edges of both ƒ holes (not at the same time even if you have three hands) while listening to the plucked sound of the strings for those higher, brighter, or duller, lower overtones. (They can also be found by tapping around the ƒ holes with the fingernail and listening to the pitches, but I find I get more information from the plucking technique.) I often plucked the second to the lowest string, although sometimes I heard more clearly and gave my ears a break by using a different string. If the violin had problems with the sound of a particular string, I often plucked that one.

After checking the sound of points around both ƒ holes, I chose the most obviously bright or dull one. If the point was dull on one side, then the point on the same spot of the other ƒ hole was extra bright. Conversely, any extra bright point had a corresponding dull sounding one on the other ƒ hole at the same place. This served as a double check since an extra dull spot was found symmetrical to an extra bright point. The spot to scrape was the dull sounding one, just as it had been for both the rib tuning and bass bar tuning procedures.

These scrapes to the edges of the ƒ holes were made with the barest touch. I used the sharp edge of a very thin knife to remove only a little more than nothing from the spot that caused the plucked sound to be the absolute dullest. As I became more skilled, the scraping was so slight that it was not enough to go through the coloring on the *f* hole edge. If the pluck was then changed to be neither extra bright nor extra dull, but rather sounded the same on the symmetrical spots of both *f* holes, it was time to locate and scrape a new dull spot.

One could continue on with this exercise until the sound of the played instrument got worse instead of better. This meant that the ribs needed tuning again. Once the ribs were tuned so that the 12 spots plucked alike and the violin sound was not improved by the addition of a clay dot anywhere on the rib spots, it was time to go back to the *f* holes and tune more points.

Nowadays, these various overtones are obvious and easy for me to hear. In the beginning this was not the case, so I was given another way to check the *f* hole points. I was told by the violin masters to hold the violin so that I was looking at its back. I did this with the scroll to my left. I was then to turn the violin in a counterclockwise motion from back to front (as viewed from the endbutton at the bottom of the violin) while placing one of my fingers at various *f* hole points to see what I discovered. It became imme-diately apparent that the sound seemed to rise as I rotated the violin for the bright points, and it seemed to fall as I rotated the violin for the dull points. I got myself another "Bravo" for hearing that one. Having this method to double check the points to tune was a, uh, Guidesend.

As with the ribs, I could put a tiny piece of clay, the size of a pinhead, on the bright spots around the *f* holes in order to determine if the playing sound got better. The clay could be used on the bright spots of the bass bar as well. However, I rarely used clay for the bar or *f* hole procedures since it wasn't necessary. Nor was it amusing to me to have the little gummy pieces of plasticene fall inside the *f* holes, which is usually what happened. I always used the clay during the rib tuning procedure in order to help me make the best decisions. At least in that case, when the clay dots fell off the ribs, they merely ended up being ground into the rug for all time—a situation far preferable to having clay globules holding support group meetings inside your violin.

Often the *f* hole tuning procedure did not need to be continued until every last bright and dull spot had become evenly bright. This was a different situation from both the rib and bar tuning in which all spots were supposed to become the same. With the *f* holes, it was acceptable and sometimes preferable to stop once the desired sound was achieved when the instrument was played.

As I rolled along with this method of tuning the *f* holes, gathering plenty of dog hair but no moss, I was given yet another way to find the most critical points to scrape. Some years earlier, Carleen Hutchins had lectured about how important it was to have the tapping sounds as similar as possible in the four quadrants of the top and the four quadrants of the back. The violin masters were now showing Marlene a pattern of tapping in the form of a "Z" on the back. They told me to notice the area that had the most dull or off tap spot. I was to continue to test this spot by tapping it as I placed a finger around different parts of the *f* holes in order to hear which area around an *f* hole fixed or improved the "thuddy" tapping sound on the back. This done, I would notice that the spot on the *f* hole, which fixed the back tap spot, was a bright spot when tested with a string pluck, and so I could scrape the corresponding dull spot on the opposite *f* hole. This fixed or improved the dull back tap.

It was the same principle that I had used in the rib scraping and bass bar tuning—an overly bright spot needed lowering with either a finger or clay. To achieve the same effect, the dull counterpoint spot was scraped to brighten it.

This alternative method of finding *f* hole spots by improving the back taps worked very well. It also gave my ears a badly needed rest from all that plucking. As the back taps became more resonant and homogeneous as a result of the *f* hole tuning (an effect that also occurred from tuning the ribs and the bass bar), the sound of the played instrument continued to improve, provided anyone else but me was the player.

I learned other acoustical adjustment techniques that were then inserted into an earlier part of the process. I'm sure I was advised of these procedures later in my training because they are so subtle—some of them are even carried out with a fingernail rather than metal scraping tools. I wasn't ready for these until after some years of practice on the less subtle procedures, which are rather subtle themselves. For example, when I was first learning the ribs, I merrily scraped away, mistakenly thinking that in order to affect an audible change there needed to be a big physical change—the removal of noticeable amounts of wood.

After several years, I gradually refined my techniques to the point where I could put the scraper in exactly the correct spot. I then removed barely perceivable bits of sawdust while effectively changing the sound. For the most part it was my thinking that had needed changing. I

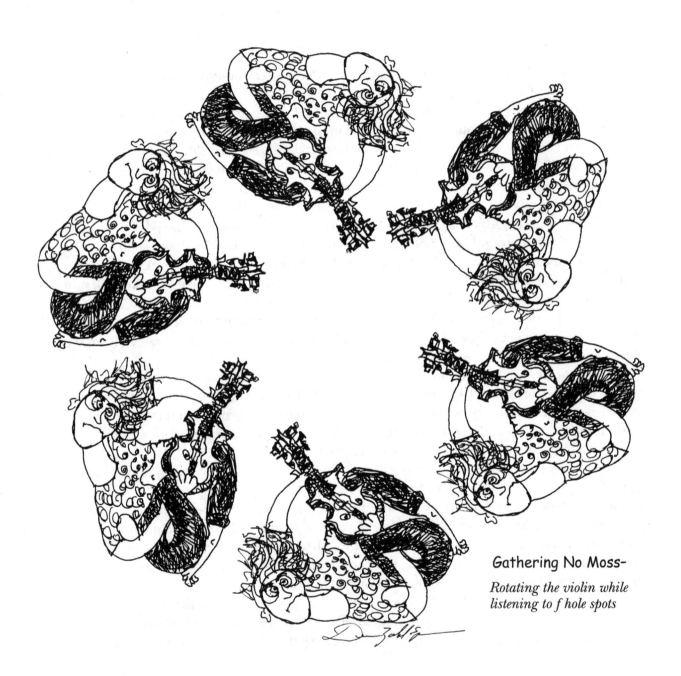

Gathering No Moss–

*Rotating the violin while
listening to f hole spots*

would not have been able to do the bass bar properly if I had tried it with the same heavy-handedness with which I initially approached the ribs. An improperly tuned bass bar, according to Guarneri, will cause a violin to sound "as an oaf or a clod."

So with ever more subtlety required, it was some years before I learned the neck and new fingerboard tuning, even though they were to be done before procedures I had already learned. This fingerboard tuning process was different from that used in the mode matching procedure described in Chapter I. It did not replace the earlier grosser procedure, as it had a different purpose.

This newest fingerboard tuning only took a few minutes to do, once I was ready to learn it. Using a knife or a fingernail as a scraper, the pitches on the fingerboard were balanced symmetrically side to side (like the *f* holes) and down the midline (like the bass bar). In this case, one barely touched the wood. It was to be performed after the bass bar tuning, the "Ears of the Angels," and just before the *f* hole tuning. It was to be done "perfectly or not at all." Oh my.

At one point during the new fingerboard tuning session, the guides referred to the "Ears of the Angels" and Marlene mentally said that she had forgotten what that was. She was told that she wasn't supposed to remember so would she kindly get out of the way and get back to channeling. This was accompanied by a ping on the back of her head. Ouch.

The subtle bridge tuning was to be carried out even earlier—before the bass bar tuning. It also involved matching symmetrical pitches from side to side. These were to be done on the sides of the bridge with a knife or fingernail, using the lightest possible touch.

Finally I was working with enough delicacy and had shifted my thinking sufficiently that I learned to tune the scroll. This was done with a fingernail and a very light swipe at the "thuddy" points to bring them up to the other pitches. The scroll was tuned side to side and down the centerline. If I had learned this any earlier, I would have overdone it. Although I learned it last, it was to be done much earlier—just before the initial rib tuning. It was then repeated in conjunction with the rib tuning.

Although the tailpiece could be tuned in similar fashion, balancing the plucked string overtones as I placed my finger on points from side to side, this was rarely done, unless the player was a soloist. There are certain characteristics of some instruments that soloists appreciate, but they make the instrument harder to play for everyone else. A cello that my husband made, which Rostropovich bought from us, seemed to be one of those. The soloists loved it, the other players, even the professionals, were less enthusiastic. It is almost like an incredible Olympic horse that can jump higher than the others, but is too much for most riders to handle.

The same instrument, like the same horse, is not appropriate for everyone. Who will be playing is an important factor to consider when making or adjusting an instrument. I was told by Guarneri to always adjust slightly ahead of the ability of the player. I guess a plastic ukulele would be appropriate for me.

CHAPTER V

A Difficult Chapter

A time of deep despair can create personal growth that we have otherwise been unable to achieve. The struggles of daily life may not be enough to break through those emotional blocks that keep us from reaching our potential. For some people, the change comes in response to a debilitating or life-threatening condition caused by an accident or illness. It may result from the process of grieving the loss of a loved one and eventually healing from the trauma of separation. I often hear or read about life-renewing spiritual development that was brought about by physical or emotional struggle. These events were horrible to live through, but many are aware that they would not have made the changes without the wake-up call.

Although few would wish to repeat pain or heartbreak, some individuals are beginning to observe and have gratitude for the spiritual evolution that was the result of surviving difficult times. Personally, I think the system is flawed. I recently expressed to my main guide my feeling that physical reality is insane. He responded that it is not the place that is insane, just the people in it.

A major shift in my consciousness (and in my energy field) came with the death of my beloved dog, Poco. I had never had a dog before Poco. By the time we were compelled to put him to sleep, my husband and I would never be the same. We were very fortunate to have had twelve-and-a-half years with an extraordinary being in dog form. There is something that can happen with an animal, where the unconditional love is so strong, and the trust so limitless, that those of us who have guarded our hearts so carefully over a lifetime drop our shields.

When Poco died, I was so shattered that the walls around my heart disintegrated. Even now, knowing I will have the opportunity to be with Poco again, I cry as I type, remembering how I felt on the day he died. When Poco left, he told us through Marlene that he was sending another dog to keep us company and that he, himself, would come back to us in a few years.

Poco

Six months later we met seven week old Yuppee Dupp—a small ball of continual motion, fur, teeth, and mischief, who grew up to be a large ball (with a sharp nose) of fur, mischief, and unconditional love. By the time we found Yuppee playing tricks on his siblings at the animal shelter, I had stopped my continuous crying. But the sudden shock of losing Poco had changed me. As I healed, I realized that my heart would never again be able to rebuild that wall, a wall that I had hidden behind for so many years. Poco's life, and his death, had prepared me for healing school.

When my husband said "no" to my request to come down to his tiny violin shop more than a quarter century ago, we almost missed meeting each other. Still clueless three years after we were married, we nearly messed up again and almost missed one of the greatest loves of our lives. Poco was born on Christmas day of 1980, one of nine puppies. His mother, Dinwiddie, lived with my brother and his wife. They asked us if we wanted a puppy. We said no. We were in the middle of building a house, we were house-sitting, we were supposed to go to Germany for a year, we . . . weren't listening.

In the course of visiting my brother's family, we did see the puppies on several occasions. There was a particular little cream and white colored one. He didn't jump and push at the barrier like the others. He sat back and quietly looked into my eyes. There was something different about him. My husband independently noticed that this puppy was somehow special.

During one of the visits, I picked up the tiny bundle of fur. We melted into each other. I returned him to the pen and we went back to our house-sitting and house-building project in Maryland, just across the Potomac River from my brother's house. (It was our first large construction project. Twenty years later my husband apparently forgot what that was like, and decided to do it all over again in New York. Some people never learn.) My sister-in-law called a few days later to say that it was our last chance—a family was coming to adopt the puppy we liked. Were we sure we didn't want him?

We went through our excuses, all quite logical sounding, all ignoring our feelings, and turned down the opportunity to have the puppy. The other family came and took home that sweet collection of fur and kisses.

Bob and I felt terrible all week. Neither of us had ever had a dog. Intellect dictated that there was no way we could have had one at that point in time. We had lots of reasons why we had made the right decision. Enough reasons to make a respectable court appearance. Enough reasons to convince a jury. Enough reasons to lobby Congress. Not enough reasons to convince our hearts. We kept on feeling more and more miserable. It didn't make sense. We didn't even know this puppy. We sure had a lot to learn.

A week later my sister-in-law called us. She didn't say hello. She just said, "Your dog is back." It seemed that the husband of the family that adopted "our" puppy had a heart attack. (We were merely having an overwhelming heartache, which none of our rationalizing was helping.) The man was recovering, but the family decided that a puppy would be too much for them, so they brought him back. Of the other eight siblings, not a single one was returned.

We are slow, but the universe gave us a second chance and we weren't going to blow it with silly so-called logic again. "We'll be right there," I told my sister-in-law. We put on our jackets and drove 40 minutes to pick up one of the most wonderful beings we could ever hope to meet.

Poco taught unconditional love (except where cats were concerned), and we needed him. I don't even want to imagine having missed him. Another close call, but we were beginning to occasionally notice when the guys upstairs aimed megaphones in our direction and turned up the volume.

Poco was a turning point in my life. He taught me how to open my heart. As he got older and began to experience difficulties, my efforts to help him resulted in learning about animal communication and finding Marlene. Without Poco, there would have been no Marlene, no healing school, and no book about how a violin maker learns to tune sound with energy.

Two years after Poco's death, I was in for another devastating departure. By this time I had completed two years of the four-year healing school and had learned all of the various physical violin-adjusting techniques that I described in Chapters I and II.

In April, guide Mary, speaking through Carla Gordan, who was in trance, told me that my father was getting ready to leave physical reality. I guess I was told so that I would have a chance to come to grips with losing him. Perhaps there were other reasons as well. I don't know. On the very few occasions that Carla's guide, Mary, has informed me that someone was choosing to leave soon, the being in question has not changed his or her mind.

Albert M. Zalkind

Although my father was 84 years old, that didn't make it any easier to hear. He'd already cheated death 12 years earlier, when the fourth heart surgeon my family had consulted decided my father's case wasn't as hopeless as it looked to everyone else. Dr. Benjamin Aaron performed a sextuple heart bypass on him. It worked. My father was quite himself even as he awoke in the ICU, immediately demanding to see all his old parts to make sure they really needed replacing. When I came to visit following the operation, I was still down the hall as I heard the doctors and nurses in his ICU room laughing. My Dad never missed an opportunity for a good joke.

It was hard enough to know he was dying, but visiting him for hours each day in the hospital during his last two months was painful beyond words. Sometimes doing everything medical science can do just to know everything that could be done has been done is not necessarily the wisest choice. The toll in human suffering can be too high. In my father's case, it was.

As a sophomore in healing school, I did everything I knew to help my father. I couldn't keep up with the drugs, the procedures, and the blindness to his condition by some of the doctors and nurses. I am not saying they all were insensitive, but it was heartbreaking that so many completely ignored the effects of what was being done to him. "You don't understand," I told one, "this man was sitting at his desk, in his office two weeks ago. Now he is hallucinating, his tongue is swollen so he can't speak clearly, and he can't think straight." They just thought he was old.

At one point, when my father's drug-induced haze cleared, he said to me. "Some day they are going to find out that all these pills are killing people." My father would have died from his internal bleeding in any case, but with each intervention 10 more things went wrong, and his suffering was both made worse and prolonged.

Despite being over-drugged, bruised, swollen, and oxygen-deprived to the point where he couldn't remember how to press the call button for the nurse, he kept his sense of humor. One of the last things he said to me four days before he died was, "So I ain't dead yet?" I concurred that he wasn't. "OK," he said, "then let's go somewhere."

"Where would you like to go?" I asked.

"Let's go to the morgue," he said. "You meet some pretty 'cool' people at the morgue." That was my father.

I was so relieved for him when he was finally free of his poor tortured body, but I was still devastated that I would never again see his grin, hear his jokes with my physical ears, or exchange a hug. I know there is no death. He knows it now, too, and he is very much with me. But the pain of those final months, and the seeming loss, was barely tolerable.

It changed me. I think it has to do with having so much feeling that it cannot be contained. It's almost as if it blasts through the body and the spirit, unjamming those places that have been frozen for a lifetime or maybe lifetimes. It can awaken emotions we have shut down in our attempt to lessen feelings of pain. When we have frozen the emotions that hurt, we are also not able to fully feel joy. Our perceptions of the physical world become increasingly distorted. The world beyond our so-called "normal" senses becomes harder to perceive with clarity. There is no select button. Energy either flows or it doesn't.

My husband took a course in college that he still speaks about. It was a class in aesthetics taught by Professor Donald Wells. On the first day of class, Professor Wells asked his new students to define "aesthetics." There was no response. After half an hour, Professor Wells asked his class to define the opposite of "aesthetics." Another half hour went by with still no response from the class. Finally the professor said, "The opposite of aesthetic is anesthetic."

An anesthetic is what is given during surgery so we don't feel anything. In order to try to protect ourselves from emotional pain, many of us adopt a kind of anesthesia, thus limiting our awareness of the entire range of feeling in multiple dimensions.

Right after my father died, I noticed that I no longer needed to touch the violin to have the overtones go up and down. The bright or "thuddy" sounds happened if I just put my finger in the air within a few inches of the area that I would have touched, but without actually touching.

Then I noticed that I didn't have to pluck the string to hear how the overtones sounded. I could feel them with a kinesthetic sense not based on physical hearing. It was something like touch, but it wasn't physical touch. I could feel mentally whether a spot would sound bright or "thuddy" if I were to touch it and pluck a string. I was able to double-check each spot by actually plucking the strings when I physically touched the violin. I had the opportunity to validate what I was intuitively feeling.

I took full advantage of this new development and repeatedly practiced listening with my non-physical senses and then checked with my physical ears. I reached inside with a scraper, and changed the "thuddy" spots, or took a small swipe with my nail on the varnish on the outside. I wouldn't be doing that much longer either.

It was one o'clock in the morning, one week after my father's death. I was lying awake in bed, absentmindedly tapping on the dresser next to me, raising the duller pitches by scraping the wood with my fingernail. Suddenly I noticed that I didn't need to take a swipe with my nail. I just had to think the change. Then when I tapped with my finger, I could hear that it was changed. I was quite startled. My husband was out of town at an architecture course, so I called my friend Laurie, who is always wide-awake in the wee hours of the night. I told her what had happened. "Yes," she said in a "no big deal" sort of voice, "that's mental healing."

I wondered if it would work on the violins. When I got up the next morning, I was afraid to pick up an instrument to try it. I did not immediately rush to the shop. Finally, I had to know. I plucked the strings of a Peresson violin as I mentally changed the overtones on the ribs. It *did* work. And the playing sound was more beautiful, just as if I had physically scraped the wood.

I got up the second morning wondering if it would still work. It did. The third morning I had my doubts again. Nope, it was still working.

It was agony and ecstasy—intense grief over my father's death and immense joy over my newfound energy tuning ability. They were trying to live together in one human body in the same moments—moments that felt like insanity.

Agony won out until I knew I was connected with my father again. It took a couple of months. Then I thought maybe I felt his presence, but I wasn't sure. Several of my intuitive friends with telepathic gifts received some of his thought communications. It was my Dad all right. Some comments came to a close family member (who wishes to remain anonymous, but to whom I have been married for quite a number of years). "Mee boy" (as my father called this anonymous person to whom I am married), "I'm going to have a long rest, I've 'urned' it." (My father's body had been cremated and his ashes were at Arlington Cemetery.) This was about on par with the morgue joke he had made just before he died. One of his groaners.

Later, this same anonymous person received a telepathic complaint from my father about the lack of restaurants in the realm where he was. He missed going to the "Big Boy" for breakfast. At the time this message was received, the in-the-closet medium was sitting and having his morning meal at a hotel on the day of my graduation from Brennan Healing Science Training. For the graduation itself, my father was apparently serious and considered it an important occasion. He said he was amazed at how much knowledge there is on earth. (This last comment came through Carla Gordan.)

In a less serious frame of mind earlier in the year, he commented to Marlene about a healing school ceremony in which I had participated. The event involved calling in the ancestors. My father remarked that it was high time he was considered a "wise guy."

One of his first communications after his death came through Marlene. It was an answering machine joke: "How to talk to God. We may not be able to get to you immediately. Calls will be taken in order. Don't think just because you are talking to God you don't need to stand in line. Joy, peace, and love." At this point, Marlene said it was hard for her to quite catch his quick one-liners and that her translation was as close as she could come. Apparently my father came right back and said that she needed a little practice on her comic timing. At which point one of my violin master guides, I believe it was Guarneri, took the opportunity to drop in and say that she didn't know much about violins, either.

I don't remember how Marlene responded, but I'm sure whatever she said, she was pinged in the back of the head.

CHAPTER VI

Thinking About the Matter of Sound

At first I did the energy tuning on violins exactly as I had done the physical scraping—one point at a time. Before starting I made sure all the seams were well-glued. I physically planed the fingerboard and matched the body tap pitch (B0) to the singing tone (Zaltone). Next I worked with the weight of the tailpiece until its resonance was in the correct place. Then I mentally raised the "thuddy" spots on the ribs, working in the same order as I had when using a scraper. Before I gained confidence, I checked the sound of the instrument after I tuned each point, just as I had when working physically.

When I was first learning rib tuning using my unusual scrapers, I removed more wood than necessary because I had not refined my technique and because I needed to believe that the sound would change only after a certain amount of material had been eliminated. This relatively gross procedure caused each newly tuned point to backslide somewhat—the just-brightened point became a little less bright after a few minutes, although it did not slip back to being as "thuddy" as it had been before the scraping.

This slipping was remedied by heading off for a quick snack, perhaps a quarter of a bag of chips, after I finished scraping a point. It only took a couple of hundred calories before it was time to check for a backslide. If one had occurred, I scraped the same point a bit more, then returned to the chips or spent a few minutes searching the cupboards for health-store junk food (I just say "no" to hydrogenated oil), in order to give the instrument sufficient time to demonstrate that it was now stable.

As I learned to scrape with more finesse, going to the exact best spot and removing barely anything, the backslide became less and less, and the price of potato futures dropped. Eventually I was just using my fingernail on the outside of the instrument, not realizing that I was already beginning the process of telepathic tuning.

When I moved to the step of using just my mind for the tuning, it was initially still labor-intensive as I searched for the most "thuddy" spots around the ribs—tuning one point at a time in the order I would have used had I still wielded a scraper. Once the ribs were completed I moved on to tuning the points of the bass bar one at a time. Just as with the physical process, when the sound of the played instrument got worse, I returned to the ribs and retuned them.

Tuning in this manner took many hours, but hours were better than days, as it had been with the physical scraping. This was fortunate, as most of the musicians who were helping me lived across the Potomac River in Virginia and needed to cross The Woodrow Wilson Bridge to get to my house in Maryland. As time went on and the hours of gridlock steadily increased, not even the closest of friends could be expected to attempt a river crossing more than once a week. If I hadn't switched to the quicker techniques of telepathy, I would never have finished adjusting an instrument.

Over time I learned that I could do the mental rib tuning by beginning at the upper bass rib and going around in a counterclockwise direction from one point to the next closest point until all the points became stable. This saved hours of time. It would not have worked using the scraper—where the points could only be tuned in the order of the most "thuddy."

After a while I learned to simply tune all the ribs at one time. Several years later my abilities developed to the point where I could tune the entire violin at once, rather than part-by-part.

The evolution of my telepathic sound-tuning skills required time to train my physical body and energy field to be able to carry increasing amounts of energy in more frequencies and dimensions. I also had to sneak up on myself so that my own limited beliefs about what was possible didn't get in the way. On the night I was absentmindedly tuning the dresser and discovered that I could change audible taps with my mind, I gave myself quite a scare. Over several years, as I moved from energy tuning individual points on a violin's ribs, which replicated the physical scraping process, to working with an entire violin at once, a change of beliefs was required. In order to progress, I had to rethink what was in the realm of possibility for anyone to accomplish, and what I, as a former self-declared psychic brick, could manage.

If you think others can do something that you cannot, the belief itself prevents you from accomplishing the task, either because you never try it in the first place or because you have blocked yourself by your belief. (This applies to everything but my violin playing—the one exception in the universe. As my dog will tell you—there is no point in my even trying to sound good.) If, as far as you know, a thing has never been done but perhaps is possible, and perhaps you could be the one to do it, at least you stand a chance of achieving your goal. It is rather like an athlete breaking a world record—sooner or later more individuals will succeed. I think this is in part because the mental barrier is gone.

As I progressed, I filled many an etheric trashcan with my discarded beliefs. I'm assuming that there is some sort of recycling program and they will not simply be wasted. Marlene continued to obtain information as I was ready for it. Sometimes I fell into the next step on my own, and sometimes I was consciously guided to it by her channel.

I was so fascinated by what was happening to the sound of the violins as I mentally changed the tap pitches, that I wondered what effect it would have on humans. I could hear that if I tapped on someone's left shoulder, and then tapped on his or her right shoulder, the pitches sometimes sounded different. Working telepathically, I found I could change the sound of taps to the human body. For example, if the left and right shoulder had different tap tones, I could mentally raise the frequency of the lower-sounding one until both shoulders matched. At first I experimented at random. How did an injured part sound when I tapped it, as compared to a normal body part? How did a stiff side of a neck sound compared to the other side?

Often a less healthy part tapped with lower overtones, although not always. If the tap were low I usually raised it. At first the effect was mild, but some people seemed to feel a bit of improvement. I got the idea that perhaps if I knew how to do more spots in a precise order, as I did on the violins, the effect would be more noticeable.

I called Marlene to see about getting information. The guides obliged and we learned that there was an order to follow when tapping and tuning a human body. Since I still had a few musician friends left, and I also had some non-musician ones whose patience hadn't even been tested yet, I launched myself into a new area of investigation. I improved as I practiced and my volunteers noticed that they felt more relaxed and balanced—until they sat in their cars at The Woodrow Wilson Bridge trying to get home. Sometimes painful areas of their bodies hurt less. For me it was the very beginning of learning to "tune" sentient beings.

I began the work by making an energy connection between the pineal gland and the navel of my human subject. This could be done by placing fingertips of one hand just above the bridge of the nose between the eyes, and the fingertips of the other hand, in the area of the belly button. (It is best to stand to the client's left side and if possible have the person face North.) Then I tapped the sides of the ribs, beginning underneath the arms, matching the pitches (tap notes) from side to side moving down, and ultimately curving around the gluteus maximus (rump). Tuning this part was apparently the equivalent of the violin ribs. The procedure could be repeated until all pitches matched.

Then the four quadrants of the back were tuned, with a tap near each shoulder and each hip. If the pitches were very dissimilar, I kept tapping until I had the desired result (or gave up). Then, just as with the violins, after each new section was finished, the ribs were retuned.

The next to be tuned was the legs, beginning at the knees, proceeding to the ankles, following with the bottom and then the top of the feet. To tune the legs, first the taps on the outsides were matched, then the insides, and finally the outside and inside with each other for each leg. Excess energy was released from each toe, starting with the little toe and ending with the big toe for each foot. Then, the ribs were tuned again.

Next the arms were tap-tuned in a similar fashion to the legs, beginning at the elbow, going to the wrist, the palm, and back of the hand. Then excess energy was released through the fingertips. Then back to retune the ribs.

Next the pitches down the back of the head and the spine were matched, beginning at the occipital bone (the bony ridge at the back of the head), and moving downward. Then I returned again to the ribs. Finally, the pitches were matched beginning at the center of the forehead, around to the back of the head, down the sides of the neck and then reversed, ending up once again in the middle of the forehead. At the end, the ribs were tuned again, just as they would be on the violin.

If one is listening to the taps on a tuned body, all pitches sound alike and are higher and more vibrant all over than they were at the beginning. One thing I learned as I proceeded was that when my heart was open, the sound of the taps was much more free and resonant than if I were just working in a cold technical way.

Just as my abilities with the instruments had progressed from changing overtones point by point to tuning entire sections at once, my work with human bodies developed in a similar manner. In the early stages of tuning humans, I had audible feedback—I could hear the changes as I tapped the areas where I was working. Later as my intuitive sensing abilities increased and my work expanded into more dimensions, this method of acoustical checking was no longer necessary.

The following is one cellist's experience with my telepathic tuning for her and her cello:

I remember as a college student that I felt the need to develop my own personal philosophy regarding my approach to life and learning (or was that a class assignment?). Anyway, I discovered very quickly that the more I learned, studied, and experienced life personally and professionally, and believed myself to be "educated," the less I really knew. The philosophical bottom line for me became: "Know your resources and keep an open mind" (because almost anything may be possible)!

Enter "the Spears." My first thoughts were related to their wonderful place in the woods, their instrument workshop, and the smell of freshly carved wood with a little varnish mixed in. Visiting Deena and Bob was like putting on a comfortable sweater. They made you feel at home and would go to great lengths to describe the whole instrument-making process. I was impressed with their scientific approach to the aging process of the wood (experimenting with soaking it in large aquariums), the exact measurements that go into the formation of each piece (of each instrument), the actual art of being able to carve the wood into the correct shape (the neck and scroll emerging from a block of wood), varnishing techniques, and then the extensive testing of the instrument with computers and sound technicians after it is made.

Once I had played three of the Spear cellos I commissioned a cello to be made for myself, one that was happily already in the making. The Spear cellos that I had the opportunity to play prior to the commission each had their unique personalities, but every single one had a wonderfully warm but also large tone. Of course, the amazing part of playing a cello is the energy or vibration that your whole body feels as the wood resonates between your legs and against your body, and the resulting variety of voices that can be produced. As Pablo Casals so appropriately said, his cello was his friend.

Well, cellos do not usually start out sounding like your friend. In fact, my cello was named Calvin by Bob, for its stubbornness somewhere along the line in the creative process. Calvin went through the scientific process, then the adjustments with Deena. At first it was tapping, putty on the ribs and fingerboard, then minuscule scrapings, and I do believe some blowing across the f holes? Playing and tapping, playing and tapping. Calvin evolved into another unique Spear creation with what I would call a very balanced, big tone. At times I thought it to be mellow while sitting behind it, but the tone sort of snuck around and could fill the room.

Deena was often keeping me up-to-date on her "healing school" and also on their dog Yuppee's growth and development. One day Deena said (after adjusting Calvin), "Why don't you let me adjust you?" My first response was, "But I'm feeling just fine." Then with a more open-minded skepticism I thought, "Well why not? What could it hurt? Maybe Deena needs to practice on somebody?"

Deena proceeded to tap (like she did on my cello) up and down my back on both sides of my spine, with a "hmm" here and a "hmm" there. She finished by waving her arms gently over my head and around the exterior of my body and off I went, through the woods, away from the Spears with a beautiful sounding cello, and I wasn't sure what else.

It was probably within an hour or so that practically everything began to seem quite funny to me, or rather I should say "hilariously funny." So much so that I was accused of being "giddy" by many of my students during their lessons. This giddiness lasted for almost two weeks and could only be attributed to dear Deena's adjustment. I might logically think that perhaps she helped me release a lot of tension in a most harmless manner. Oops, hope I didn't laugh at any of you!

I have been fortunate to keep in contact with Deena as her healing skills have continued to grow in the most unbelievably believable ways. I say, "Hearing is believing." I recently called Deena thinking that perhaps my cello had come unglued after a rigorous summer of outdoor concerts in the heat and humidity with a lot of air conditioning mixed in. Deena answered the phone with a soft, slightly broken voice and said, "I'm really too tired tonight to glue your cello over the telephone." I had previously had my cello adjusted over the telephone, but the gluing part was another remarkable prospect.

I proceeded to again visit Deena in person to discover with the actual physical testing that my cello was not unglued. Deena was rested and she once again moved her hands gracefully up and down my instrument, plucking the strings, looking and listening, feeling something with a very intent look on her face. The cello mellowed, it brightened, it aged, it again became modern. It eventually balanced high and low. What can I say except, "Thank you Deena! You are an invaluable resource!" My philosophy lives on: Keep an open mind, anything is possible!

Barbara Van Patten
Professional Cellist and Cello Teacher

Having the giggles for two weeks is just one of those surprising things that can happen as a result of healing work. The giggle-aftermath healing was relatively early sound work on humans for me; I was still tapping and listening with my physical ears. As for the long-distance work that Barbara mentioned, the development of that is described in later chapters of this book. What with Congress still fighting over The Woodrow Wilson Bridge, long-distance work became a necessity in the D.C. area, even with my local clientele.

CHAPTER VII

Live and Don't Learn

C hakras are vortexes that are part of the energy fields of people and animals. I was surprised to learn that musical instruments have them too. Energy comes and goes through these vortexes. Although not visible to physically focused eyes, chakras have been common knowledge in oriental medicine for centuries. The practice of acupuncture utilizes the various meridians and vortexes that form an energy grid, which supports the human physical body.

These healing practices that utilize unseen energy pathways, while still considered "alternative medicine" in the Western World, are gaining credibility. If acupuncture, which works on principles of a kind of energy that scientists currently can't measure, is becoming acceptable, can energy instrument tuning be far behind? Well, yes it can. Perhaps I can prop the door open a crack with this book and allow a slight breeze through. I suspect I'll be viewing the entire affair with amusement from my ringside seat in heaven before this art becomes as common as changing a string.

The information that instruments have chakras came through Marlene, who has the ability to see them. There are seven basic chakras on the human body. The first, called the root chakra, has its tip at the base of the spine on the end of the tailbone. Barbara Brennan's book, *Hands of Light* goes into this system extensively. These chakras are numbered in order going up the body. The seventh has its tip pointing at the crown of the head.

I learned that violins (violas and cellos) also have seven main chakras on the body of the instrument. As with humans, there are other chakras, which are not on the body but rather are found beyond the area where physical matter appears to end. For bowed string instruments the first chakra is at the top of the scroll. The seventh chakra points to the endbutton.

It was time for me to work with the energy field of the violin in ways that had no physical equivalent. When I asked Marlene if there were some procedure that could be performed physically that could replicate energy work on the chakras, she heard hysterical laughter. When the clamor died down Guarneri informed me that *"the farther one gets from the physical, the closer one gets to the music."*

At this point I was in my third year of healing school. We were engaged in healing all seven chakras on humans as part of the curriculum. I was passing my skill tests and feeling reasonably confident. At home, I'd been successfully changing violin tap pitches with psychic energy for quite a number of months.

I was informed that tuning *instrument* chakras required more talent than I had previously used in a healing. In addition, the higher the chakra (for example seven as opposed to one), the more its energy increased in frequency and strength—demanding ever more ability from this would-be violin healer if I wished to effect a change. One doesn't just start training for a 26 mile marathon by simply running as fast as one can for 26 miles on the first day out. We are speaking of someone who is in his or her right mind anyway. It takes time to build up the stamina of the body. Learning to work with ever more gentle and refined, but at the same time more powerful, energy is a process similar to building athletic endurance. When I was told about the chakras on the violin, I was also warned that they were different from human chakras, and that on the violins I was to practice doing the first one and not more.

I did practice doing the first chakra only. Yes I did. Unequivocally, unquestionably, beyond a shadow of a doubt, yes—for a time. I should be given a little slack here as I was living in the energy of Washington, D.C. where the meaning of yes depended upon what was meant by yes. I meant "yes for four instruments."

As a child, I didn't want to see Walt Disney's version of Dukas' *The Sorcerer's Apprentice* a second time. Whenever I saw *Fantasia* I focused my attention elsewhere for that part. When the sorcerer left the castle, his novice apprentice, Mickey Mouse, took the master's magic wand and began commanding the brooms to carry buckets of water so he didn't have to lug them himself. Mickey soon lost authority over the energy and the situation quickly spun out of control. Before long the entire castle became flooded. I couldn't intercede and stop Mickey from creating disaster so I didn't wish to undergo the discomfort of viewing the story again. But decades later I evidently decided to do my own reenactment—casting myself in the role of Mickey. It was an excellent choice.

Miss Impatience. I wanted to practice tuning a few more instrument chakras, but I had already done the first chakra on all of the instruments in the house. There weren't any more. If there had been more I really would have focused on doing only the first chakra as instructed—maybe. So it wasn't my fault. There were extenuating circumstances. After all, the pursuit of knowledge is noble, and say . . . what if I just try tuning all the chakras on this one little old violin to see what happens? Just this once?

"Wrong Deena."

Did I hear whispering in the ether?

"WRONG DEENA!!!!!!!! You heard yelling in the ether, mixed in with some Italian swearing."

But of course I didn't hear anything. So I proceeded to do my Mickey Mouse version of tuning all seven chakras. Well, it wasn't exactly working. Actually, it wasn't working at all. The instrument was sounding steadily worse. So I tried harder. I pushed, I pulled, I strained, I— suddenly noticed that I had a very uncomfortable feeling between my eyes. Sort of an ache in an area where I'd never felt anything before. It really hurt. How could that be?

That could be because you just fried your third eye.

Oh.

So I discovered my third eye. Yes, I'd read about it in metaphysical books but I'd never actually been aware of it in my healing and energy work. I was definitely aware of it now. Ow!

The third eye, also known as the pineal gland, has been written about for its mystical powers for centuries. It wasn't that I didn't believe in it. I had just never thought about it. I was thinking about it now and it finally became clear to me why the violin masters had said I was "a diligent but trying student."

A few healing sessions with Marlene to work on my pineal gland, a whole lot of Italian yelling and swearing in Marlene's head, a number of grapefruit for Marlene, and I was ready to resume work.

This time I was careful not to go past the first chakra, but I was not careful to stop working when clients and instruments kept pouring out of the woodwork. I felt obligated to get them to sound good. One person had an audition. Another person had a recital. The *coup de grace* was a cello, which, even under the best of circumstances—and they weren't—took much more psychic energy at that time than a violin. I was really pushing it.

Energy sound tuning is best done with a relaxed, gentle, loving feeling. The energy flows to create the beauty of sound. It can be an exhilarating experience reminding me that it was more than worth whatever the costs of pursuing this art. At that moment, however, I was not reminded of anything except the possible need to pursue a different line of work. I was exhausted and desperate.

"Stop, Deena."

"Huh?"

"STOP, DEENA!!!!!!!!!!"

"Did you hear something, Yuppee?"

"Woof!"

"Well, I've just got this one last cello to do. It's our cello. This player has a recital. I've got to get it sounding good."

Grunt. Push. Strain. Push! Push!

"OWWWWWWW!!!!!!"

That ache between my eyes was back.

Uh oh.

My next session with Marlene was like a post mortem. "We're collecting your molecules from across the universe," she said. This time I needed more than a dozen healings on the pineal gland as well as a vacation of two and a half months from performing any energy work, including healing on humans.

They say that when you die you see the film of your entire life. I hope they serve a jumbo-sized box of popcorn—with butter.

The secret

of energy-tuned

varnish

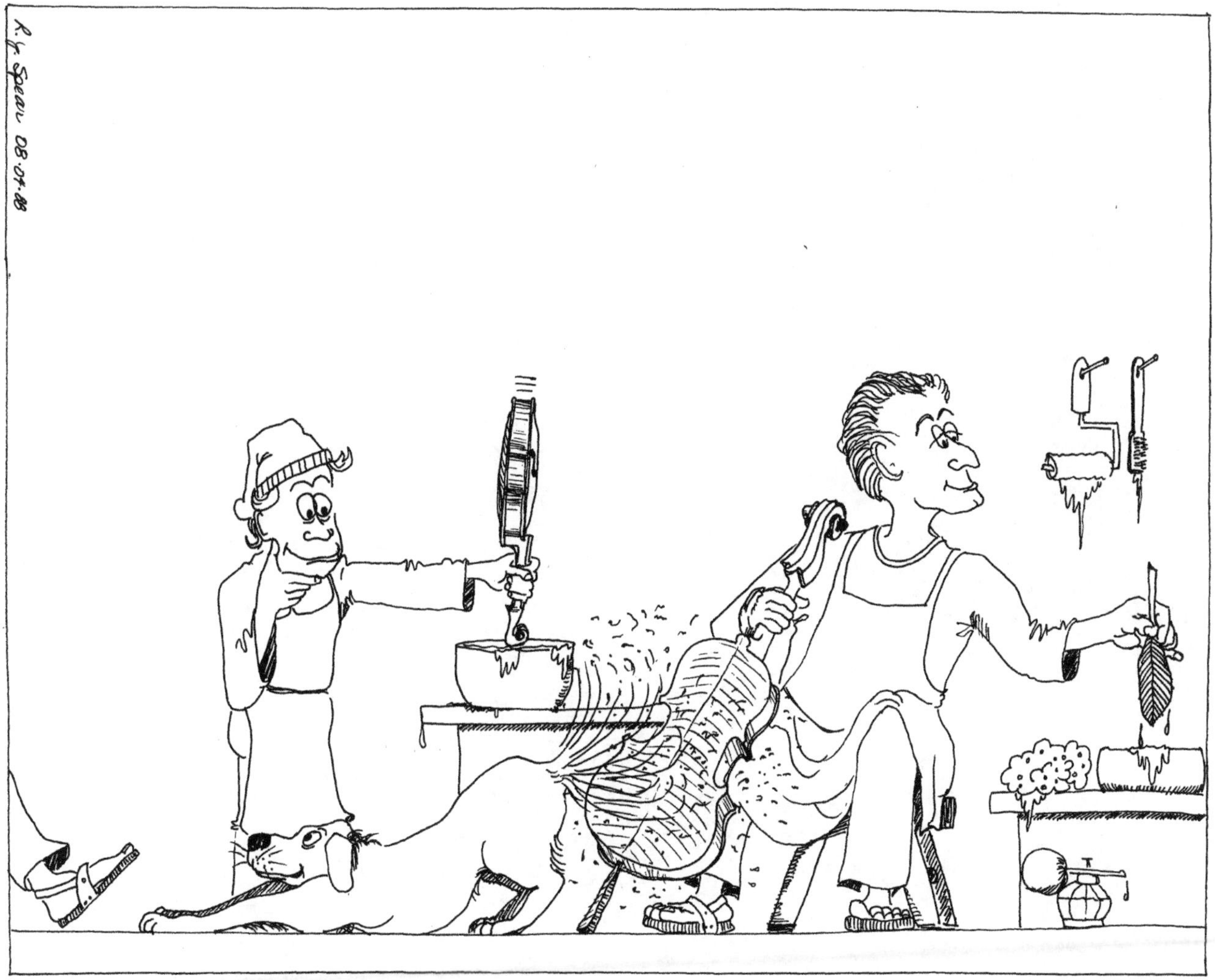

CHAPTER VIII

Sorry, Tinkerbell— I Never Believed in You

❧

There was never any shortage of things to do while I was resting from energy work. For one thing there were still discoveries to be made in the physical realm of violin making. Those tailpieces that had driven me to consume mass quantities of fruit-juice-sweetened gluten-free cookies were far from mastered. I knew what frequencies I was aiming for, but hitting the target, let alone the bull's-eye, was another matter. I didn't know what I needed to ask. Fortunately it was one of those times, like the "Ears of the Angels" tuning procedure, when the guides volunteered the information without a question from me. Probably they'd heard about as much whining as they could stand. I've often wondered if they were assigned to me as some kind of penance for earthly misdeeds.

À propos of nothing, I was told to tap the tailpiece not only in the center as I had been doing, but also to the right and left. I couldn't imagine why they had given that instruction; however, "diligent but trying" as I am, I proceeded to tap to the right and left as well as the center of each tailpiece that I was tuning. Eventually the fog lifted and I realized that when I got a clear ring all the way across, the thing was tuned. Any double pitches or dull thuds on either side, not just the center, meant that I hadn't gotten the tailpiece quite right. Considering how critical the tailpiece is to the sound of the played instrument, and how tricky it is to find the best frequency for it, this was a big breakthrough.

Marlene channeled other information of interest to those of us who try to turn small pieces of wood into instruments for the expression of the human soul. For example, although some violin makers know that the edge of a violin *f* hole functions best if it is an even thickness all around, I hadn't really thought about it.

The violin masters pointed out that some of my instruments, and some of the other instruments that I was adjusting for other makers, had quite a selection of thicknesses on each *f* hole. This was hurting the sound. They went on to remark that 2.7 mm of thickness (as was specified in Simone Sacconi's book *Secrets of Stradivari*) was indeed usually the best choice for the thickness of the entire edge, but there were exceptions. Then they gave the new information that if a violin is for a great soloist, it's best at 2.65 mm. They added that 2.8 mm is optimum for a beginning student. (Sort of like a slower, gentler horse for a child, I guess.)

I checked my instruments and, yes, there was something for everyone—but unfortunately it was all on the same *f* hole. I don't know how they see this stuff. Guarneri gets impatient with me when I try to talk metaphysics. For a disembodied spirit, he sure is a hands-on kind of guy.

I evened up the *f* hole edge thicknesses on several of my instruments. The differences in sound were not small. With the consent of the other makers whose instruments I was also adjusting, I improved the *f* hole edge thickness situations and found a similar improvement in the played sound.

My vacation from healings gave me the opportunity to remember questions that I hadn't thought about when I was focused on the energy tuning. Depending on the topic, we sometimes still needed to speak to the guides individually as they didn't always agree. It was predictable that when I inquired about the acoustical difference between a long style Guarneri *f* hole and a shorter Stradivari design that both Italians would emphatically voice very different opinions. They did not disappoint. Poor Marlene, it was another three-grapefruit day.

She was much happier when we had agreement from all the guides since it was easier for her head. Topics such as sealers inside and outside the instruments were fortunately among those on which all parties agreed. In fact, in the matter of the inside sealer we had several hands-on sessions with another violin maker, who has decided to subject the work to study with scientific equipment. So I will not get further into it in this book. I will say, however, that ultimately it has become possible to create the effect of some of these physical recipes by using energy only. It is convenient that this energy work may be performed after it would be too late to work with the physical materials.

Also important during my down time from energy healing was to focus on my mental and emotional evolution. As a part of Brennan Healing Science Training, the students were required to be in therapy every two weeks during each of the four school years. When I began the program, I felt impatient with the school for having so much emphasis on the study of personality. We worked extensively on self-examination—our wounds and defenses and how we projected our wounds onto others, coloring our perceptions of the people in the world around us. When was our intent negative? How had we hidden this from ourselves? What was the awakening process they kept talking about? I just wanted to learn energy techniques. Wrong, Deena.

Learning to observe ourselves honestly and without judgment, and working with those characteristics that need transformation is a full time job. Anyone evolving as a healer carries increasing amounts of energy. This means that the good, the not-so-good, and the awful aspects of a healer's emotional make-up also become energized and magnified.

To know oneself better, to recognize one's negative intent and one's own control issues is paramount if one wishes to be as pure a healer as possible. To not recognize one's own issues while attempting to help someone else heal is a recipe for disaster. Not only is the client not helped, but also I have observed the self destruction of some talented healers because their egos became large enough to get stuck in the doorway.

The process of self-awareness and transformation is and has been a slow and sometimes painful one. Much to my surprise, when I began to get help from the violin masters, many issues that I had never considered arose in me.

As a child I had been Little Miss Realist. I never believed in Santa Claus. When my older brother and older cousins teased me and said they had x-ray vision and could see right through me, I knew they were full of it. Now, decades later, I was in the process of learning real magic. But Little Miss Realist was still stuck inside of me. She kept me safe, or so I mistakenly believed. I wasn't going to be anybody's fool. She had protected me for years, but like many of one's childhood defenses, she was getting in the way.

There was literally an energy block across my diaphragm and through my solar plexus. During a therapy session, when I asked myself about this stuck energy, I recalled scenes from the x-ray vision teasing of childhood. I hadn't thought about that in a very long time. To me it was a symbol of not wanting to be gullible or thought of as gullible. Yes, it was true that the other children had no x-ray vision (well actually, they really did, but didn't know it), but to limit one's thinking as a general reaction to avoid being considered naïve, or maybe even crazy, was not a good remedy. As open as I was, I was still limiting myself, and that was going to limit my development and my work.

It might seem that being a so-called realist would keep one grounded. However, being grounded, having a connection to the earth that keeps one from mentally floating off into space, has nothing to do with whether or not one retains a material view of reality. Grounding is what allows one to do energy healing and intuitive work without acting like a new-age flake. Some people who consider themselves realists are simply closed-minded—a condition that results from fear. You cannot be in fear and be grounded at the same time.

I never believed in the tooth fairy. But the stuff I was now learning to do with mental energy seemed no less fantastic, only it wasn't a fairy tale. If I stayed with what many others believed to be a realistic view of our world, then I limited my thinking too much and I was going to miss the real music.

I also needed to work with feeling worthy. Why me? Why was I privileged to get this information? A piece of that was the pesky self-love issue—loving myself and allowing myself to be loved. It is important, it is a piece for most everyone, and I'm still working on it.

I made progress in the emotional work, so when my third eye was healed enough for me to resume working with energy, I found that my skills had improved. It didn't come all at once. It was, and is, a step-by-step process, but I don't usually make the same mistakes—I constantly find new ones.

I was ready to continue my education in the tuning of chakras on instruments. This time I cautiously added only one chakra at a time as I learned to carry stronger energy in more dimensions. It was like being rewired. If you are a wire rated to carry 120 volts, it is unwise to try carrying 220 volts until the new lines have been finished and you have been approved by the electrical inspector. When I got ahead of myself, I've been lightly sautéed to deep fat fried. The personal work is a big part of that rewiring process.

As my chakra tuning skills grew, I got closer to eliminating the need for the physical "mode matching" procedure—the process of planing or shortening the fingerboard so that the body tap (B0) would match the Zaltone. Ultimately, a very well tuned instrument can go without "mode matching."

It took me several years of chakra tuning practice, but I finally managed to achieve this state in a viola. Although the body tapping pitch and the singing tone (Zaltone) had begun as notes that were a minor third (three semitones) apart, after my best yet chakra tuning job, an entire range of notes became resonant when I sang into the f holes—from the original body tap note to the original Zaltone, including all the notes in between. Also, the whole body tap (B0) then rang, which it normally did not do unless the body tap and Zaltone had been physically matched (usually with fingerboard work). The instrument sounded wonderful.

I learned that one of the important things that our modern violins are missing is the quality of wood that the old masters had. Energy work was not needed back in the late 1600s and early 1700s when Stradivari and Guarneri created their masterpieces. Because of the qualities that the wood had in those times, and the energy and skill of the masters themselves, the instrument chakras were automatically tuned, and many remain so today.

Apparently the sort of energy work I am learning can bring back the kind of quality of sound more frequently found in those Old Italian masterpieces. Our industrial society and resulting pollution have done much to alter the trees. There is a limit to how far we can redeem our modern compromised wood by purely physical means such as soaking the raw wood or using different "thicknessing" schemes. As people realize that believing in this kind of work is not like believing in Tinkerbell, and as more individuals learn to consciously alter energies mentally, we will be able to have a larger number of good and great instruments. Some of our best instruments are now 300 years old, and they will not last forever.

I came to finally understand the secret imparted to me by the first intuitive, Fred Mansbridge, whom I had consulted on the matter of violin sound. Touching the wood with loving kindness was not like believing in the Easter Bunny after all. It was about transformative energy. Not only does the energy vibration of love change sentient beings, but it also alters wood and its resonance so that an instrument truly becomes an extension of the heart of the musician.

CHAPTER IX

Reach Out and Touch Someone— Anywhere, Anytime

*I*t is one thing to accept the possibility of energy work when it is hands-on, but quite another to believe in its effectiveness over a long distance. I had the opportunity to both observe and experience long-distance energy healing before I had even contemplated studying healing myself. In one case, I had sent a lock of my dog Poco's fur to John Payne, who at that time was alive and living in Ithaca, New York. Poco had been having back problems, which disappeared shortly after John received the fur and performed a long-distance healing on him. I didn't know why it worked, but the timing of the sudden recovery certainly indicated to me that the healing was likely responsible.

Later, after meeting Marlene, I had the chance to experience a detox (a process to lessen or eliminate harmful effects) from dental anesthetic. I had been feeling extremely tired for the two weeks following an injection of Novocain. Marlene performed a long-distance healing as we were on the phone. The change in how I felt was immediate and dramatic—my energy was back.

Barbara Brennan, in her second book, *Light Emerging*, gives an excellent explanation of why distance healing might work. According to recent thinking in physics, the universe is a hologram. Each part contains every other part. An entire hologram can be reconstructed from a tiny piece of it. This means that if you have a holographic picture of a frog, and you remove a piece that's just one of its toes, then you have the picture of the entire frog again in the small piece that was the toe. Each piece carries the information for the entire picture.

When I tune into a person's energy field, I am locating a particular vibration—a unique signature that is a part of a universal hologram, which all of us have in our unconscious mental address book. I just need a key to be able to touch into the energy of the being that I am seeking. It has been my usual practice with an adult human to initially make the connection by listening to the sound of his or her voice, because I am sound-oriented.

If I am working with an animal, I ask the human companion to think of him or her and then I can immediately contact the energy field of that animal. I also locate the energy fields of children and babies by having those who have contacted me—usually a parent or relative—think of them. I can also tune into a being's vibration from a photograph. Some healers use a lock of hair in order to connect.

When working in the dimensions in which energy healing is performed, there is no distance. This fits with the holographic theory of the universe. I can't tell whether someone is in the next room or half a world away. Once I am connected with a person's field, we are together, and space does not exist. It is all simply a matter of focus—like switching to a different frequency to change the radio station that you are listening to. Whether you wish to hear Mozart and Beethoven or The Doobie Brothers and The Grateful Dead, you don't need to leave your house—just turn the dial or push a button, depending upon the age of your equipment.

Working with healing energy, whether in person or long distance, can physically change whatever or whomever you are working with. It is the harmonic induction principle of one vibration creating a like vibration in a receiver. If the receiver is a person or animal, the change in the energy will only take place by agreement, conscious or unconscious. When first learning long-distance healing, it can take some time to adjust to the fact that you are actually able to locate, connect with, and affect the particular energy field of your intention.

I was lucky to have the opportunity to work with instruments, because they offered clear validation of my long-distance energy healing abilities. At first, even though I believed in long-distance healing, I wasn't so sure I could change the audible sound of a violin that was not in my hands, let alone not in my part of the country. I had run into the iron bars of my own limited thinking. However, there's nothing like a little desperation to motivate a jailbreak.

Roberta Crawford is an instructor of viola at Binghamton University in upstate New York. She had (and still has) a viola that my husband made for her. I had set up her viola and had been keeping it adjusted when Roberta could make the eight-hour drive to Maryland. For many years the adjustments were physical, but as I began to replace my scraping techniques with energy work, I shifted to using the energy instead—but only in person when I could hold the musical instrument myself.

At one point, something happened to the viola—it suddenly sounded terrible. Roberta had an upcoming recital and no time to drive to D.C. This event took place before I had learned long-distance healing (also called absentee healing) at school, as that skill was not taught until the senior year. Confident, I wasn't.

I was not very far along in the instrument tuning procedures at that time, either. I was still working with individual points rather than changing the whole instrument at once. I asked Roberta to play a scale over the phone while I listened. Then, as I described to her the various spots to touch on the ribs, I asked her to pluck the strings of the viola near the phone receiver so I could hear them. When the points sounded low, I tuned using the same process, as I would have in person.

I heard the overtones of the points shift. So did Roberta. After all the overtones of the 12 points sounded about the same, Roberta played again. Success! The sound was just as if we had been working in person. However, my nerves were just as if I were eight years old again and having a memory lapse while playing "I'm Called Little Buttercup" on the multipurpose room stage of Patrick Henry Elementary School, ending forever the musical performance career I could have had if only there had been some talent.

The viola was making progress. Next we did the bass bar. Roberta touched the points along the top above the bar and plucked the strings as I listened and mentally tuned the ones that sounded "thuddy." We were able to improve the viola enough that it sounded good to Roberta. I could hear the change as she played her instrument, even though I was listening over the telephone. What a relief!

As I have become more sophisticated in my ability to enhance instrument sound with energy, the long-distance work continues to be every bit as effective as working in person. However, I still prefer to have the opportunity to physically adjust the fingerboard and tail-piece frequencies before using energy on an instrument that I am "tuning" for the first time.

Although I am approaching the point of being able to make up for an incorrect tailpiece frequency with energy, I like having the physical set-up correct as it saves time and effort and may still yield better results at least part of the time.

Up until now, it has seemed easier to tune the instrument chakras hands-on. Fortunately, they usually only need to be done once. I believe that my preference for doing the initial chakra work in person will probably change. At the moment, an instrument that has been physically mode matched, has a good tailpiece frequency, and has tuned chakras, is as easy, if not easier, for me to adjust telepathically over the phone. Perhaps my energy work will get to the point where seeing an instrument in person for initial adjustments will not be necessary or even helpful.

The ability to work long distance has been a tremendous relief, as my husband and I have clients all over the country whose instruments I can keep adjusted without any of us leaving home. But to accept that the sound of an instrument is changing, when no one is physically present to change it, is quite a mental and emotional leap for most musicians—even for the ones who have experienced and believe in hands-on energy work. How could I expect any different? I, myself, had a bit of a belief gap. Frankly, if I weren't doing this all the time, I'm not sure I would consider it possible. I might be the one thinking that the person claiming to do this work was two quarts short of a gallon.

Bonnie Cohen of Alexandria, Virginia contributed the following:

> I was on a job playing my viola for a wedding and mentioned to one of my violinist colleagues that I had just gotten a beautiful violin made by Deena Spear. The violinist grew rather quiet. She looked uncomfortable. Finally she spoke. "I've heard some very strange things about Deena," to which I replied, "Trust me, no matter what you've heard, she's much weirder than that."
>
> "Well . . . " the violinist continued, "I've heard that she heals instruments by laying her hands over them!"
>
> "Oh no," I chuckled, "She doesn't do that anymore. Now she adjusts my violin and viola over the phone."
>
> By the look on her face it was clear that was not the reassurance she was looking for.

Violist Ellen Olson of the Jacksonville Symphony purchased one of my husband's violas before any of us knew that my adjusting techniques, while already innovative, would become science fiction material. (Yes, this is the same viola I wrote about earlier—the one that had the near death experience. It wasn't through with me.) As time went along in the way that it appears to us mortals, I began to use hands-on energy work in order to adjust all our instruments, including Ellen's viola. While it did seem strange to her, she coped. As I began to do the long distance work, I saw no reason to mention it, until I got a call from a very unhappy Ellen. She lived in Florida, a 12-hour drive from Maryland, and her viola was not sounding or responding well. It was beginning to remind her of her old viola:

> *I remember calling Deena very upset over it and she suggested a telephone adjustment. My heart sank. "Oh no," I thought, "Deena's lost it." I remember calling Philip and asking him what he thought of the whole thing. He told me that I had nothing to lose and that I should try it. But the idea was totally nuts to me. I remember making long-distance calls to other musicians that Deena had worked with over the phone. They all told me—try it! But it was just too weird. Finally, I asked my friend Jeanne, who knew about Deena, if she might play my viola and do the tuning with Deena over the phone for me. That first time I was totally amazed. I kept asking my husband if the sound was really better or was I imagining it. He agreed—the viola sounded better. Still, it was too much of a stretch for me to do it myself. I remember taking my viola over to Philip's house and leaving it there so he could call Deena and do the telephone tuning.*

Eventually, it became inconvenient to have Philip Pan (Jacksonville Symphony Concertmaster) do the phone tunings for Ellen. And it became clear to me that Ellen's energy was so much a part of what was happening with the viola that it was important for Ellen herself to be the player:

> *. . . But when you get desperate, you keep trying things. Eventually, after I bugged Philip several times, Deena gave me one of her great pep talks about coming from a place of joy and taking responsibility for my own instrument. I finally got up the courage to do it*

myself. Believe me, it's still weird, but I cannot deny the fact that my viola sounds better after most of the long-distance tunings.

Notice that she said, "Most of the long-distance tunings." Ellen, like Roberta Crawford, has an energy field so connected with her instrument that the sound can be indicative of how she feels. I had one memorable long-distance tuning session with Ellen during which I tried for over half an hour to budge the sound of her viola and almost nothing was happening— except exhaustion on my part. I was totally frustrated (not the right state to help resolve the situation), and couldn't understand what was going on.

I had tuned several other instruments long distance that week. They all had adjusted quickly and easily. We decided to try again in a few days. This time the viola sound changed within a few minutes to the lovely rich tones we knew were possible. At the end of this session, Ellen remarked that she had been in a very bad mood during the previous session. From now on, I will only work with Ellen's viola when she is in a good mood.

Violinist and violin teacher Lisa Cridge describes her experience with long-distance energy tuning:

An awful thing happened to my violin. I was practicing for my next concert when the phone rang. I had been expecting the call, so I jumped up and placed my modern Italian violin in its case, which was perched on an extra chair. I unfortunately didn't fasten the Velcro around the neck and didn't shut the case. As I picked up the phone in another room, I heard a 'meow' and a horrible crash. I ran back to my practice room, and discovered with horror that my cat had jumped up in such a way that the lid had shut on top of the violin. Both the instrument and the case had flipped over and landed upside down on the hard floor.

I stared for a long moment, afraid to even imagine the damage that had been done. Finally, I prepared myself for the worst, and gingerly lifted the heavy case off my pretty violin. I sighed with relief, however, as I discovered that everything seemed intact—no scratches, no cracks, and no rattling soundpost. After a while, I settled down to finish my practicing. I was ready to hear my instrument's warm and colorful bell-like tone. As I drew my bow to the strings, I grimaced as my ears were positively assaulted by the piercing, screaming sound. It was thin and really ugly. It hurt my ears, especially when I played the E string. The bottom of the sound had apparently been knocked out of the instrument, and what was left sounded worse than a factory-made child's violin.

I knew that something had to be done immediately to help my fiddle to recover from the fall. I called Deena, as she had worked on my violin in the past and I recalled that she had a good reputation for fixing and adjusting traumatized instruments. Even though I knew she had experimented with 'non-traditional' methods of instrument repair, I was quite surprised when she told me to stay home, stay on the phone, and hold my instrument in my lap. She asked me to periodically pluck the strings, and I wondered what she was doing during the periods of silence that I heard. She apparently was doing 'something' though, because I noticed the strangest thing, the sound of the strings was changing. She then instructed me to play the open strings with the bow, and finally to play a G major scale. Every time I would play, we would both comment on the quality of sound. Then there would be a pause, and I'd play again.

Even though I had considered myself an open person, I was skeptical. I knew that the sound was getting rounder and deeper, but I wondered if somehow I were manipulating the tone. After all, it was in my best interest to have a great sounding instrument. I knew deep down, though, that something really miraculous was happening.

After I got off the phone, I stared at my violin. I had just had it adjusted long distance! I decided I'd better keep it a secret or my friends would surely think I had gone whacko! But then I started getting compliments. Most people said that I had just blossomed as a player. One demanded to know who had adjusted my violin, so I came out with the truth—it was Deena Spear, and she had actually improved the sound long distance. This particular friend knew my violin well, and looked at me in disbelief. He kept saying that it didn't make sense, that my violin just couldn't sound that good. He walked away scratching his head. Another friend was a little more open to new ways of thinking, and so she then had her viola 'worked' on by Deena. She was very happy with the result.

All I can say is that what started to be a horrible accident has been a wonderful experience for me and for my violin. Sometimes, apparent tragedies are gifts in disguise!

Lisa Cridge, Principal Second Violin, National Gallery Chamber Orchestra
Washington, D.C.

What about instruments where glued seams had become open? When I dealt with open or weak seams, before I began using energy, I found it useless to do any of the usual adjustments, such as moving the soundpost. Even the scraping procedures did not work when the seams were open. If an instrument were not sounding right, I could do nothing for it until it was glued. How was I going to deal with that one long distance? I didn't know.

I had to wait until my skills were ready, but there was also that small matter of belief again. Marlene assured me that I could do this: the seams might still look physically open, but when the energy was fixed, the sound would change. Either she was five musicians short of a quartet or this was going to work.

First I practiced gluing seams with energy in person, hands-on. Well, the instruments did, in fact, sound as if they had been glued after I did the telepathic work with the intention of having them energetically glued. This was getting curiouser and curiouser. By the time I was learning this, most of the musicians who owned our instruments knew what I was up to (although there were a few who were left blissfully ignorant). This afforded me many opportunities to interact with various players and experiment with a number of instruments. I needed to convince myself that I wasn't making this up. Eventually, I believed my ears and the musicians' ears; I accepted the irrational obvious. Then I tried it long distance, and it worked. I improved with practice.

As I got further into healing work, I learned to stop analyzing every little thing. I had to observe, even if I didn't understand. If something worked consistently, it worked; and all these long-distance tunings worked. Now it is routine procedure.

Most of my violin clients are and were professional musicians. Most had no interest in energy work. They just wanted beautiful sounding instruments. If they didn't have to drive for a day or two in order to have their instruments adjusted, so much the better.

When I lived in the D.C. area, almost all my local clients eventually saw the wisdom of staying home and calling me on the phone. Aside from The Woodrow Wilson Bridge, mentioned earlier, negotiating the Washington, D.C. beltway can turn into a different trip than originally planned. As I was writing the first draft of this chapter, there had been four major beltway incidents in just that week—from overturned trucks spilling gunpowder across the highway, to enormous blocks of ice in the middle of the road (in the middle of summer, because they had fallen off a truck).

As I am editing this chapter, which I wrote nearly two years ago, I am now living in Ithaca, New York where one can reasonably estimate the time a local trip will take. However, because of its four-page comic section, I still get *The Washington Post* newspaper, so I have not lost touch with the "ebb and ebb" of D.C. traffic. If you are coming to our nation's capital—and plan to travel by car—pack a lunch.

But I have digressed—and it was worth it. I had been writing about how I continually have to unlimit my own thinking in order to expand my abilities. The musicians who work with me must also go through some sort of acceptance process. Most manage to do this because their physical senses tell them that their instruments are resonating in a very different manner after an energy tuning session. However, I am sometimes amused to hear the rumors flying around and how adamantly people defend their perceived realities. They don't want to hear that things could possibly be any different than they have long believed them to be.

I knew that violinist Leslie Ludena had been unprepared for the reception she got when waxing enthusiastic about my work several years ago. I asked her if she would write up her experiences for this book. She sent me the following:

I have taken my 1986 Peresson violin to Deena Spear for repairs, adjustments, and fine tuning ever since I acquired the instrument in early 1987. Over the years I've been extremely pleased with the results, and I trust Deena's opinions and judgment. So when she started to develop unusual methods like scraping very small amounts of wood from inside the violin, and some years later, changing the sound with energy, I was willing to investigate.

My experiences watching Deena and hearing the effects of her work have impressed me immeasurably. I can't imagine my violin sounding better than it does. Many times I have participated in the adjustments to my own instrument as well as to the violins in her studio that belong to others. I'd play for Deena from across the room and then we would discuss the need for improvements in such things as balance, power, and the general quality of higher or lower registers. Deena would make some changes based on our mutual observations, then she'd hand the instrument back and listen to it again as I played.

For several years these adjustments were done with her scraping methods. Then she made a switch to using only energy. During these energy sessions, I was amazed to hear the specific changes that we had discussed after watching Deena work on the violin without picking up a single tool. We would hand instruments back and forth for hours at a time, which gave me an opportunity to observe the entire process on more than one example. I don't fully understand what she does, but hearing the sound and feeling the difference in how the instrument plays has convinced me that it works.

In 1995 I joined the Kennedy Center Opera House Orchestra, and I quickly became aware that many of the string players there felt that Deena Spear ought not to be trusted to work with instruments because of her "hocus pocus" ideas. Rumors had spread that she was involved in "some kind of new-age stuff" and that to allow her to make any adjustment could be "dangerous" to an instrument. I soon learned that all of the players expressing these opinions had NEVER played violins altered with Deena's unique procedures. I tried to defend her for a while with depressing results, and I eventually avoided any discussion on the subject with my colleagues.

After three years at the Kennedy Center, I won a position in the San Francisco Opera Orchestra. Since going to work there, several members of the committee that selected me from the audition have said that they were particularly impressed by my sound, inquiring about my violin. So far I've been reluctant to disclose the "new-age hocus pocus" secret I believe to be greatly responsible for the continuing maturation of the power, clarity, and sweetness of my instrument, which draws so many complimentary comments. These favorable observations have only served to strengthen my belief in Deena Spear's work, particularly when a problem is corrected using only energy, either in person or long distance. I hope that more musicians will open their minds, explore her energy techniques and hear the outstanding results for themselves. I still look to Deena when my violin needs help, and I expect that she will continue to develop the energy tuning and share it with players and makers who are willing to listen.

Leslie K. Ludena
Violinist, San Francisco Opera Orchestra

As my friend Marianne, who is reading this manuscript as it is being written, has commented, "Few would think you are other than marbles rolling around in an otherwise empty loft."

CHAPTER X

A Chemical Concerto

❧

The more I tuned the instruments, the more validation I had, and the more I learned. When the energy field felt a certain way, it sounded a certain way. As the musician played the instrument after each energy adjustment, I had many opportunities to feel the field and then to hear the sound.

As I practiced the ability to feel the silent sound of an instrument, the intuitive kinesthetic sensations became almost as clear as physical touch. For example, some of my perceptions of silent sound were like having my hand in flowing water, some felt more like slow moving tar, and others had the texture of a pile of gravel—the last being something that I didn't want to hear aloud. The education I was receiving from the instruments helped me to trust that my healing work on humans and animals was also creating more harmonious sound because I could feel the changes in the silent vibrations as I worked. In addition, once I knew that I could alter sound on instruments hundreds of miles away, I felt more secure about the effectiveness of my long-distance healing work with sentient beings. The violins were wonderful teachers.

Working in silent sound dimensions lends itself to many different kinds of healing. One of my specialties has become detoxing—mitigating or eliminating toxins. From a sound perspective, if someone ingests, inhales, or is injected with a substance that has a harmful effect on the body, the resulting sound is not a beautiful one. It would be like trying to listen to a Brahms concerto with one ear and a heavy-metal rock band with the other. It may be stereo, but it's not a happy mix.

The sound which results from a toxic substance in a human or animal body feels to me to be a jarring and inharmonious beating of vibrations against each other. This creates a disturbance in the energy field, and, ultimately, damage to the physical body. If one transforms this vibrational interaction into something that is more harmonious, then the chemical is no longer toxic, or as toxic.

The validation that I have succeeded in creating greater harmony between chemicals and bodies has come in many ways. For example, I had a client who had been poisoned by Dursban, a chemical pesticide used for termites, which unfortunately was also an ingredient in a flea and tick powder that she had used on her cats. Among her symptoms—from which she had suffered for the four years since the use of that powder—were frequent, and sometimes severe, dizzy spells. I focused on her energy field and perceived a very unpleasant, thick-feeling sound, which I believed to have been created by the chemical still held in her tissues.

I performed a long-distance healing on her for about an hour. Because we were on the phone, at the end of the session I asked her to sing individual notes so that I could listen with my physical ears to the frequencies that still needed help. I tuned the vibrations that I could hear were not resonating well.

When I spoke with her again, about two months later, my client said that she not only had been pain-free for five days after the healing, but her dizzy spells had *never* returned. More work was needed so she could learn to be in the new habit of no pain, but the initial detox apparently had a permanent effect. I asked my client, Gia Miele, to describe her experience in her own words. She sent me the following for this book:

In 1997, I had an episode of vertigo, which resulted in hospitalization and recurring bouts of dizziness and loss of equilibrium. Like so many ailments, it finally took an intuitive to read my body and diagnose my condition. She saw that I had been overly exposed to a chemical, which was affecting my neuro-transmitters. She recommended I contact Deena Spear for a harmonic healing. Even though I am a strong believer in alternative health and healers, consulting with someone who tuned bodies like violins was a stretch for me. But I called her and we had a session. For most of the hour I did nothing and said little. Then I had to sing notes for her to tune my energy. When she made corrections where needed, I heard notes come from my throat that let me know, in every cell of my being, what a perfectly tuned instrument felt like. I have never felt dizzy or loss of equilibrium since that day.

When I work with animals who have reactions to vaccinations, or who have had too many vaccinations at once, the change after a healing is often quick and obvious. In the words of one client, Lucyna Staryzyak: "After a series of vaccinations, my cat, Whisper was lethargic and had lost her appetite. I asked Deena to perform a long-distance detox. Just as soon as Deena was finished, Whisper began to play and eat. I could tell she felt much better."

Observations of the aftermath of two surgeries, performed less than a week apart on the same dog, offer further validation of the value of long-distance energy support and energy detox work:

Tiki, my Yorkshire, had surgery to remove a mast cell tumor growing on her back left leg/hip area. She came home from the surgery very disoriented from the anesthesia. For several days she fought the negative effects of the drugs. I could tell it made her depressed and agitated. Finally, on the fifth day after surgery she started returning to her typical positive mood. It was at that same time that we learned that not all of the cancer cells had been removed. She needed surgery again.

My friend suggested I call Deena to help Tiki remove the anesthesia toxins from her system. Deena worked long distance with Tiki in advance of the surgery, immediately after surgery, and for several days afterwards. In addition we used some homeopathic remedies. The experience was remarkable. Tiki was more tired than disoriented when she came home the day of surgery, and by the next morning her eyes were clear and she was getting back to being her true self. She recovered within a couple of days—it was like a 180-degree shift from the first surgery less than one week before. The energy work also had a positive effect on myself and my other dog, Tiger—a close companion of Tiki since she was a puppy. We were all grateful for Deena's healing work—it made the difference in Tiki's recovery.

Cynthia W., Virginia

Dental Novocain is another one of those substances that can wreak havoc in the auric field and the body. Before learning about energy detox, I used to become extremely tired and out of sorts for several weeks following a visit to the dentist that involved getting an injection of one of the "cains." There are various formulations including Xylocain and Lidocain. I found that those mixed with epinephrine increased the side effects in my body. (Although everyone reacts differently, I eventually found Carbocain with no epinephrine to have the least side effects for me.)

I remember hearing Barbara Brennan describe watching her own auric field split in two as she was given an injection of painkiller at the dentist. Often clients notice a big and immediate difference in how they feel before and after an energy clearing of this substance. As the healing work brings back beautiful sound, the clients say they feel better and have their energy back.

Some clients can physically assimilate only a bit of change at a time. I may feel that the sound of an energy field has improved, but the person or animal may experience recovery more gradually—integrating the shift in the energy field at a comfortable rate for him or her.

A transformation—for the better or for the worse—that will occur in the physical body appears first as a change in the auric field (and can be observed by an intuitive who has the talent for this). This alteration of the energy field, in turn, affects physical matter. When I tune the sound of an energy field, I am helping to create a more harmonious vibration both to prevent illness and to help recover from it.

I have spoken with a university professor who hopes to develop equipment that would be sensitive enough to pick up some of the changes in the energy field of the human body, and could be used as a part of medical diagnostic techniques. The physical body vibrates, but at a slower rate than its energy field. Vibrations in the energy field affect the vibrations of the physical body.

If I take a tuning fork, which vibrates at the note A when set in motion by tapping it against a hard object (such as my head), and if I attach this tuning fork to a hollow block of wood (not my head), that tuning fork would vibrate audibly whenever I play the open A string on the violin. This is a process called harmonic induction. Barbara Brennan's book, *Hands of Light* has a detailed discussion of harmonic induction and how the vibrations of something like toxic thoughts in the energy field literally become physical; the mental vibrations influence the slower vibrations of physical matter, such as the human body.

I was fortunate to have both my experience from years of instrument tunings, and opportunities to observe the outcomes of healings in which the results were clear. All of that has helped me trust my ability to judge silent sound. This is especially important, since some results of healing work can be difficult to confirm.

One hard-to-validate result is the changing of the vibration of mercury amalgam in the teeth. Mercury vapor can be measured in the mouth of everyone who has these types of fillings. Mercury does not have a positive effect on the human body. For some sensitive souls, it appears to have contributed to serious illness. I have read of various cases in which some individuals have had their fillings removed and then subsequently recovered from illness or had relief from debilitating symptoms.

Small amounts of mercury, while not an asset, are handled well enough by a number of people, and detoxed by the appropriate organs. For those whose health appears to be adversely affected, getting the fillings removed is not a walk in the park either. It involves creating more toxic fumes, and being injected with a fair amount of Novocain—with its exaggerated toxic effects in a sensitive person.

As I became more familiar with tuning sound to alter the vibration of toxins, I began to think about the possibility of diminishing or eliminating the side effects of mercury amalgam in teeth. I read the books of specialists in the field of mercury amalgam toxicity and talked to them by phone—without actually explaining what I had in mind, so as not to have them think I had tripped too many breakers in my electrical panel.

I researched various ways of measuring the amounts of mercury coming from the teeth, including the use of a mercury vapor meter, measuring amperage (current), measuring potential difference (voltage), and measuring mercury in blood and urine samples. Each expert disagreed with the opinion of the other experts as to how these measurements were best made accurately. This was going to be tough to validate scientifically. Unless I had one of those dramatic cases, where the major problem was the amalgam, it would not be so obvious that there really had been a change resulting from the vibrational healing work. In addition, I might be changing the vibration of a chemical so that it did not react in such a toxic manner with the body, but it still might register as the same chemical in a scientific test. I had to trust my abilities to feel the silent sound and know that the mercury and the body were resonating in harmony after the healing was complete.

I discussed my ideas with Marlene. She thought detoxing should be possible for fillings and spent some time intuitively looking into the matter. Eventually we got together in person.

She revibrated the fillings in my teeth. My mouth felt very different—much lighter. I also brought a tooth with a mercury amalgam filling that I had obtained with much difficulty. It was one of those situations where the American Dental Association continues to insist that there is no danger from having these fillings in your mouth, but the restrictions for disposal of these teeth are so severe that you are not even allowed to take home your own mercury amalgam-filled tooth, should the dentist pull it out. It is perfectly safe in your mouth, but not on your shelf? Hello? You are just kidding, right?

Although I do not consider myself to be a psychic, I am now going to put my hand to my third eye, roll my other two eyes as far upward as they will go, flutter my eyelids, and make a psychic prediction: Once the practice of putting mercury in people's mouths has vanished, scientists will make the startling discovery that the stuff was, after all, toxic and should never have been extensively used as a major ingredient in dental fillings. Furthermore, it will be ascertained by a committee of people with many Ph.D.s that all those fillings have ended up in the soil and water as a result of being inserted into the teeth of most everyone in the Western world for many decades. However, a different group—a well-funded one—will declare that these elevated levels of mercury in the environment are not that big of a deal and are "naturally occurring" anyway, so standards of contamination levels tolerable to humans will need to be adjusted (to allow for more mercury), since a cleanup will be too expensive and have too big of an impact on "The Economy." Now, where was I?

I performed my first mercury tuning on this hard-won little piece of toxic waste. (I hope this does not put me at risk for incarceration by the dental amalgam police.) Changing the vibration of mercury amalgam was not a particularly fun procedure, but I felt that it was something that, if it could be done, should be done. Most people whose fillings I have vibrationally altered have felt a difference, just as I did. I didn't particularly encourage my clients to hire me for this procedure, as it used to take me quite a while and was very tiring. As my work progresses, this procedure is becoming faster.

To my knowledge, I have not had a client whose major disease symptoms were caused by mercury amalgam, so I can't report any dramatic cures. It does feel to me, however, that after my sound-healing work the vibrations are changed and that the material in the fillings is no longer inharmonious. If one were able to find some reliable method to take mercury measurements, I would guess that at my current level of healing ability (which I assume will continue to improve), the tuned fillings would still register as mercury. To find a method to measure the changed toxicity would be useful, but I haven't seen a scientifically acceptable way to do that.

A friend built me Hulda Clark's "synchronometer," a device that measures electrical resistance and is dependant upon the skill of the operator. That piece of equipment showed that people who had undergone my mercury healing procedure no longer tested as if they had toxic mercury vibrations in their bodies. However, I'm not sure I could stand up in front of the National Academy of Science and convince those folks of the synchronometer measurements, or my sanity for that matter.

Perhaps there will come a time when measurements are more sophisticated and the changes in toxicity obvious to the scientific community—of which I was once a member. Violins are difficult to measure also, and a violin resonating more beautifully is still a violin. I've been an acoustical researcher for a long time. The best tests of instrumental sound are the human ear and the musician's perception.

One well-known violin acoustics researcher, who was retiring, told a story about how the musicians would insist that their instruments played and felt very different, even when the scientific equipment kept measuring no change. Finally, the researcher came to believe the musician, and concluded that it was time to develop better equipment. Trying to measure the results of a detox healing, as well as other healings, presents similar challenges. If the client feels better, this can be indicative of success. With something as subtle as a change in the vibration of tooth fillings, scientific proof is problematical. Like the musicians, I must trust my own ears, in this case—psychic ones.

Having the ability to work with vibration is good news and bad news. The good news is that I and others can offer effective help to those who need toxicity removed from their bodies. The bad news is that if the healer is not grounded enough, among other things, he or she can learn just how real this energy stuff is.

The first time I used healing energy to help clear some of the toxic side effects of chemotherapy, I learned the hard way—again—that the manner in which I was working needed a few modifications: *Be careful what you merge with, Deena.*

"Huh?"

I had waited 24 hours after my friend's chemo treatment, so as to not interfere with its efficacy. This is the instruction I was given because that worked best for my skill level at that time. (I have since changed techniques, which will be explained in a later chapter.) Then I proceeded to touch in (long distance) with the vibration of the chemicals and transform the sound into one that had greater harmony with the body. This completed, I went about my business as usual. I felt fine.

A couple of days later I decided to wash my hair. I was rubbing the shampoo into my scalp when I noticed that large clumps of hair were staying in my hand because—I surmised after deeply pondering the matter for 10 seconds—they were no longer attached to my head. The more I washed my hair the more this happened. I stared in disbelief at fistfuls of hair. I knew this was a side effect of chemotherapy, but I had never had chemotherapy; I was healthy, had not taken any drugs or eaten anything unusual. The only thing I had done differently was to clear the vibration of the chemo from the energy field of my friend—who still had *her* hair.

"Oh."

Someone flipped one of those circuit breakers to the "on" position; I was pretty sure I knew what had happened, although I was still somewhat amazed. I talked to a few intuitive friends and was given confirmation: I had apparently taken on some of the chemical vibration myself.

Marlene gave me some suggestions about using grounding (connection to the earth) that allowed for more flexibility. I got the idea to imagine the feeling of an ice skater who could move in different directions while his or her blades were still firmly in the ice. Over time, I became more experienced in detoxing clients from these kinds of chemicals (without merging with their vibrations—the clients' or the chemicals')—and haven't had a repeat of the incident. Those events were a different kind of validation of the reality of vibration and energy fields, and one of those lessons I will never forget. The hair on my head grew back—and unfortunately, everywhere else as well.

Still more proof came in other ways. I have been testing and measuring violins for a number of years, with assistance from various individuals who are more equipment savvy than I am. In recent years I've gotten considerable help from my friend Alexander Thornhill, a retired electrical engineer, who got stuck with us after falling in love with our first dog, Poco, and then our second rascal, Yuppee Dupp. Alex spent much of his adult life inventing electrical devices and performing various tests and measurements for the Naval Research Lab.

We decided to measure the "Q" of unvarnished violin tops and backs, which were not attached to the rest of the instrument. "Q" is the amount of ring or resonance of an object when vibrated. For example, a bell has a much higher "Q" than a concrete block or a package of two cream-filled Hostess Twinkies.

In order to measure "Q," we placed an accelerometer in the center of a violin plate (top or back). An accelerometer is a very light device (ours weighed 0.5 grams), which senses a change of velocity, yielding data about frequency and amplitude of vibration. We placed the accelerometer in the center of the violin plate in order to study a particular mode of vibration, known in violin acoustics as mode 5, or the ring mode. (It is so called because if you sprinkle glitter on the unattached violin plate, and then vibrate it with the correct note for mode 5, the glitter will form a circular pattern. The frequency that forms this ring shape is also the note you hear if you pick up the violin plate and tap it in the middle.)

The plate was vibrated by hitting it close to the center with a small hammer. This hammer, which itself contains an accelerometer, has become known—following a considerable lack of discussion—as an accelerometer hammer. Hitting the plate with the accelerometer hammer triggers the computer to read the output of the other accelerometer, which is affixed to the plate with some sticky stuff. The computer collects and stores the data from the accelerometer on the plate and calculates the frequency content of the vibrations by a method known as "fast Fourier transform."

Much to my joy, both the hands-on and hands-off energy work measurably changed the "Q." I tapped around the plate with the intention of raising the pitches. I could hear them rising. When we tested the "Q" for this procedure on various different plates, we saw that, using mental energy, I was able to raise it between 5 and 7 points. When I tapped with the intention of lowering the pitches (which felt very uncomfortable, since that was not an improvement for the wood), I was able to lower the "Q" about 2 points.

I decided to see what would happen to the "Q" if I did a procedure on the wood that was not in the order of my usual energy protocol. At the end of a healing on a person or a violin, there is a "sealing" of the work, which is accomplished in a high frequency range. This sealing procedure should be carried out only after the entire healing is complete. In this case, instead of doing the sealing after the plate energy was at its best, I reversed the order, performing the sealing procedure after I had intentionally made the sound worse by lowering the tap pitch.

The results amazed me. The "Q" fell more than 8 points—heading in the direction of the Hostess Twinkies. I had not physically touched the plate. I believe I had forced an incompatible situation and set up a jarring beat frequency in the wood, making it much worse for use in a musical instrument.

This last result of the inharmonious frequencies interfering with the resonance of the violin wood may have some similarity to a situation when a chemical is not compatible with a human or animal body. I believe it also shows what happens when we push and force things with our will, instead of using our hearts and allowing for what is needed.

CHAPTER XI

A Musical Medley

The body's initial reaction to the creation of more harmony in its energy field is unpredictable. My clients often tell me that they are less tired, have more energy, and sleep better at night as a result of the healing. However, shortly after a healing or the next day, it is not unusual to hear that my client felt as if he or she had been hit by a truck. Over time the body integrates the more harmonious vibrations and then the person feels better—often much better than before the healing. Sometimes the body has a reaction, which assists in clearing toxins.

One of the healings I performed apparently caused a prominent skin rash, which appeared quite suddenly less than an hour after the end of the session. My client was chemically sensitive and had inhaled a toxic amount of an exterior house preservative. She had been feeling ill for days prior to the healing. Although the skin rash took some time to disappear, she felt well the day after our appointment, and much better than she had for weeks. In other situations, I have tuned clients where the intention was to clear rashes that were already there. In many of these cases, the rashes then disappear—instead of appear.

After a healing, many clients feel much better—more cheerful and more optimistic. However, an emotional detox may instead be among the first effects of healing—a positive result, despite how it looks. One example of such a response was a client who cried uncontrollably at frequent intervals for days following the healings. It happened at work; it happened at home; and it happened at moments that she considered to be quite odd. Each time we had a long-distance healing session, the initial symptoms were the same—a couple of weeks filled with intermittent tears, which made no sense to my client. However, once she was through the "emotional detox" period, her chronic physical pain was greatly relieved.

When a person initially feels worse rather than better after a healing, this is called a "healing crisis." It is like clearing a pipe that has mud-caked walls. At first the water becomes turbid as the mud is loosened from the sides and mixes with the flowing water. The dirty-water effect is temporary. Eventually the mud clears from the pipes, and the water becomes transparent again. The pipe is no longer clogged with mud and has a greater diameter of open area available to carry more water flow. In healing, the physical toxins (the equivalent of mud) may come out through the digestive system as diarrhea, or on the skin as a rash. Previously suppressed emotions such as anger, grief, or joy may be released. Often the toxic energy may transform as a part of the healing, leaving the lucky client to simply feel better.

One client, whose blood pressure was already elevated, had a sudden rise in the pressure on the day following the healing. After that, the pressure dropped to a level lower than it had been, and it stayed there. The intuitive reading from Carla Gordan on this situation was that the healing had released the boundaries around my client's suppressed anger, which created a temporary rise in the already high blood pressure (healing crisis). The "held" anger was responsible for the high blood pressure in the first place, but once the healing work released the trapped toxic emotion, the blood pressure was able to fall to a healthier level.

I can't predict the response that a person or animal will have when I have completed a healing. The manner and rate at which more harmonious vibrations are accepted into the physical body is not up to me. This is the client's choice, although not necessarily a conscious one. A healer sets the intention for the highest good and then proceeds to facilitate a flow of energy to fulfill that intention. Trying to force a particular outcome is the same as trying to control another's life, and a sign that the healer's ego is in the way.

Sometimes a healing is not accepted or integrated into the energy field, even though the client may have requested the session. People have many reasons, both conscious and unconscious, for not getting well. The issues behind ill health are often complex and go far beyond physical causes. Healing energy can touch deep levels of vibration where thought, emotion, intention, and belief affect the formation of the physical world. Healing at these levels can reach the root cause of the problem to help change a client's hidden agenda or conflicting beliefs, which are preventing good health. Healings assist in giving someone options. The extra energy and particular vibrations make it easier to accomplish more harmony in body and spirit if that is the path chosen.

Under some circumstances, death can be a healing, and is sometimes the choice that a client makes. It takes energy to die—to make the transition from physical reality to spiritual reality. A healing is performed to offer the person or animal the energy that can be used to proceed to the next step with less struggle, if this is the wish of the one receiving the energy. The being could also use that same energy for any purpose he or she chooses.

Sending healing energy is offering help, not forcing someone to accept it. It is like giving people musical instruments and offering to teach them to play, but not beating them over the head should the instruments or lessons be declined. It is not our place to judge another's decision. We don't know all the factors.

It can be difficult, if not close to impossible, for a healer to let go of the outcome of a healing, particularly when it comes to working with close friends and family (including and especially animal companions). The kind of work I do, working with silent sound, requires that I be in a relaxed and loving, but detached, state. The violins have taught me exactly how things sound when I become tense while doing a healing—they scream. The shrillness of an instrument that results from my being emotionally wound-up is most unpleasant to hear, even when played by a good musician.

There are forms of energy healing where healers can still be effective even if not at their own emotional best. That may be less so for the kind of work that I do. I must get into a sense of pure love, while letting all else go during the healing session. (There is always time for stress later.) Occasionally I haven't succeeded in reaching this blissful, open-hearted state. Panic can be so insistent when you are too close to a situation.

Every once in a while I encounter a client whose field feels like concrete to me. These people are not ready for an entire healing and must be worked with a little at a time, if at all. When I have ignored this warning and instead tried to push, pull, and shove the energy to move blocks and create more flow, I have found myself to be a physical wreck afterward—the unhappy result of using will (personal ego).

If a healer's serenity has vanished, and he or she finds himself or herself taking a jackhammer to the energy to try to force a client to accept a bigger change than that person is ready to handle, then it is time for the healer to take a rest. Engaging in a battle of the energy fields—the healer vs. the healee—is not a good idea. I would like to think that I now have finally learned this lesson, after forgetting it every now and again. Pushing energy is so very human and last time I checked, alas, I still was one.

In my work I have seen many conditions relieved quickly. Severe headaches caused by allergic reactions are often among these. A detox healing to change the inharmonious inter- action between the offending substance and the body can frequently alleviate the stress in a short period of time.

An example of another condition, which shifted quickly, was that of a young man who lived in Paris, France at the time. His mother, who is a friend of mine, became very concerned about an infection and swelling in the arm of her then 25-year-old son. Since my friend resides in the United States and could not be there to help her son personally, she called me to see if I could do something. I didn't have the opportunity to hear his voice, so I located his energy field through my friend's thoughts of him. She also faxed me her son's photo. Unfortunately the fax looked more like a series of ink blobs than a human being. Neither the distance to Europe, nor the ink blobs, mattered.

Her son, like everyone, is in the universal holographic "Rolodex." I used her thoughts of him to locate his vibration. Since energy healing work is performed in dimensions in which space (distance) does not exist, for all I knew he might have been sitting in the next room instead of lying asleep in his bed in France. Here is that portion of an e-mail from my friend's son to his grandfather, which describes his experience of our non-physical healing encounter:

On another subject, I would like to tell you about a rather surprising experience I had recently. A week and a half ago, my right elbow became infected because of a cut which I had not cleaned properly. It swelled up, became painful to move in any way, gave me a fever, and showed no sign of getting better. Mom was worried enough that she had me go to the emer- gency room just to be sure I didn't require immediate medical attention. It turned out that it could wait until the next day, when I could see a doctor, but the physician in the emergency room thought that I might need minor surgery to reduce the swelling. I wasn't very pleased.

When I called Mom back upon returning to my apartment, she said she had asked a friend of hers, Deena, to work on me while I slept. Apparently, this woman can work on patients at long distances, somehow being able to sense their energy. I don't know much about how it works, but I do know that when I woke up in the morning, I felt significantly better, and by the time I went to the doctor's office the following day, it was clear that I no longer needed medical attention.

Now, perhaps my body was able to take care of this injury by itself, and that was all there was to it. But it was just getting worse and worse until the night that this woman worked on me, so I think she might have had something to do with it. It is very difficult to understand how this might be the case, but I don't see any other direct reason for my improvement. I thought I'd let you know since her services may prove useful to you. . . .
Josh Levy

In other situations, changes in the energy field may not be physically noticeable until a little bit of time has passed. When working with cancer, I channel or direct the energy to tune the sound. People or animals who have cancer, or any illness, have their own agendas. The outcomes of these healings are less a reflection of my work and more an indication about choices the client is making. Sometimes a healer or intuitive can help a client understand the thoughts behind a condition in order to help the client make a different choice.

In one case, my client was a free-spirited, elderly cat who was quite clear about what she wanted. She felt she still had work to do in her physical body, she was not ready to die, and she used the healing energy I sent accordingly. The human companion of the cat sent me her description of events for this book:

After 20 years of living a very independent life of chasing moles, squirrels, and chipmunks out of the yard, my cat Keke began to slow down and chose to stay in the house more. In October of 1998, she began to limp. I thought she had caught her nail in the rug, so I called the veterinarian promptly. The vet determined that the cause of the limp was a mast cell tumor/round cell tumor and infection on her left rear middle toe. The vet prescribed Prednisone, Depo-Medrol, and Baytril. I called Marlene Sandler, with whom I had worked before. At the end of the session, Marlene suggested that I call Deena Spear to "fine tune" my cat's condition.

I did just that. When Deena began to do healing work with Keke over the phone, Keke decided to sit in my lap. This was highly unusual as she normally is much more independent.

I felt quite surprised. After the healing, the condition began to improve and I began to gradually reduce the dose of medication. Unfortunately the tumor reappeared. I called Deena again. After this second healing, I started backing off the medication and this time the tumor completely disappeared. I stopped giving Keke the medication altogether. The next time the vet came to check Keke's paw, she spun around and said "What have you been doing? I have never seen cancer heal like this!" Months later the same veterinarian and her partner, who had also examined Keke's foot when she had the cancer came to my house to see my dog. During the visit they also checked all of Keke's paws. The one who had not seen Keke since the healings, exclaimed, "This is amazing!"

I know there is more to Keke's story, and I want to thank Deena and Marlene for showing me another way to heal.

Jean Ward

Working with animals is always interesting and frequently rewarding. Almost all my animal healings have been long distance. In an earlier chapter, I mentioned a cat named Whisper who had made a quick and obvious recovery following a detox healing for the bad effects of multiple vaccinations. Shortly after that healing, I received another call from Whisper's human. Here is Lucyna's description of that event:

A few days after the vaccination detox I asked Deena if there was something we could do about my relationship with Whisper. My once very affectionate cat had become aloof since she was spayed a few weeks earlier. Again working long distance, Deena assisted Whisper in releasing her anger and tuned the relationship cords between us. After twenty minutes (we were on the phone), Deena said the energy felt harmonious. Whisper immediately ran up to me, jumped in my lap, let me know she wanted to be petted and started to purr. This is something she had not done since her spay operation. Whisper continues to behave like her old, playful, affectionate self.

Lucyna Staryszak, Maryland

When I started the relationship tuning described above, I had the intention to assist in the release of Whisper's anger, but only with her agreement. As soon as I began to send the healing energy, Whisper began to run and jump around in a crazy manner, according to Lucyna, who was sitting and watching her. Lucyna said Whisper appeared to be going berserk for about the first 10 minutes of the healing. Then Whisper left the room where Lucyna was on the phone with me, and took herself downstairs to the basement. She reappeared just as I was finishing and immediately began to snuggle her human after weeks of being emotionally distant. No other healing on Whisper has created this frantic behavior. Perhaps as I was helping her work out her anger energetically, she was working it out physically. I don't know.

Whisper

Another client who showed a quick response to a long-distance healing was an elderly female cat with a sense of humor. Shortly after an hour-long session, the cat suddenly jumped up on the bathroom sink and playfully swatted her surprised human, who was engrossed in washing her face and hadn't noticed the airborne feline. This was behavior that this cat had not exhibited since her health had declined. After the healing, the cat appeared to be feeling better. In this case, healing sessions were repeated, as she seemed to need them.

I have also tuned relationships between family members. The parents of a friend of mine were having difficulties relating to their two daughters and their grandson. After a long-distance tuning at the request of one of the daughters, all the relationships became far better than they had ever been. My friend and I were both astonished at the large shifts that took place. The free will of each individual is always involved. However, tuning the sound between people, or people and animals, can have a profound and permanent effect. It seems as if the release of discord in the sound of the energy field helps some people and animals to let go of fear, open their hearts, and free the natural tendency to love.

Normally, I do not work on a person unless I have their request or at least their consent. When tuning the energy of a relationship, if one party has requested help, I consider it ethical to tune the relationship *between* the party who called me and the other person who is involved in the uncomfortable relationship. In my opinion this is not the same as working on someone who has not consented to healing work.

In the following long-distance healing, when I began to tune the relationship *between* a husband and wife at the wife's request, the husband, who does not believe in the sort of work

I do, absorbed a great amount of energy himself. Evidently, on the unconscious level he very much wanted a healing. He was not, and is not, conscious that any of this took place. At the beginning of the healing, I felt that his energy was not grounded in his body. By the conclusion of the healing work, his energy field seemed to be fully in his body with a beautifully tuned and expanded sound.

Several weeks later I received a call from the wife (my client) with wonderful news. The change in her husband was so striking that I requested she write up her experience for this book. She sent me the following:

> As promised, here are a few notes regarding the energy healing that you did for me. Feel free to write it the way you want. The important thing is that your work with me was so very successful.
>
> As you know, initially I called you for an energy healing for my cat who had twice been at death's door with a liver infection. When I saw the wonderful improvement that he made at the time and is still enjoying, I was convinced that I should call you to help me resolve an ongoing problem of my own. I was having shoulder and neck pain, which I felt was directly related to unexplainable and inappropriate outbursts from my spouse, which I always felt were fear-based. As soon as an outburst happened, I could feel the pain roll up my back into my shoulders and neck.
>
> During my energy healing with you, I became so tired that near the end of your work I was literally lying on the floor while listening to you on the phone. After I hung up the phone I took a three-hour nap! And I am not a person who naps during the daytime. From then on my shoulder and neck pain never returned under the above-mentioned circumstances. That has been a great relief and comfort to me! The very next day I had an opportunity to put your work to the test, and to my great relief the shoulder and neck pain did not appear as it had before we worked together. The following day my spouse began to change dramatically.
>
> Because of the 'other' work that you did for me that day (Deena, I'll let you tell about this part in your own words), I haven't had an opportunity to test it again because of the extraordinary and wonderful healing that took place with my husband. Here are some wonderful changes that I've noticed:

Characteristics before and after the energy healing that took place that day.

1. *Very withdrawn and quiet.*

   AFTER: Now he is very talkative and seems to feel more free to express himself. Smiles and laughs a lot. He has become a real "Love Muffin" and expresses love and affection and tenderness that I have never before seen in him.

2. *Nervous and fidgety.*

   AFTER: Much calmer and is sleeping a lot better.

3. *Gulping food at meals.*

   AFTER: No longer gulping meals and eating frantically.

4. *Moody and sad.*

   AFTER: I no longer see the sadness I used to see all the time. He looks 10 years younger and smiles all the time. His depression has disappeared completely and things that would have at one time bothered him no longer seem to matter. He seems to have a lot more energy.

5. *Poor eye contact.*

   This always bothered me and now he makes good eye contact.

6. *Arrogant, defensive and fearful*

   AFTER: These characteristics have changed dramatically and over all he is much happier with himself and his life.

What a miracle to have this wonderful, loving person in my life. One of the most comforting things you told me was that he probably never knew how he was hurting me. Just knowing that has made it possible for me to let go of the pain involved with his old behavior. Also, I have noticed that as he heals, I too, am doing some healing of my own. I also expect that as this part of his being is now so different that some aspects of his physical health will also improve. In the meantime, I am forever grateful to you, your work, my Universe, and my Creator. Please let me know if you need or want any more information.

   B.L., North Carolina

Sometimes I haven't altered the outcome of an illness, but appear to have made a difference in the quality of life. Shortly after I began healing work with one dog, who was dying of cancer, she began wagging her tail and asking to go out and play. She hadn't shown either of these enthusiastic behaviors for a while. The dog eventually died from her tumor, but seemed to be more comfortable and happier in her final weeks.

I have had a number of clients who have been able to substantially reduce their pain medications once they have undergone tuning work. In one case, a wheelchair-bound client was concerned about the amount of morphine and another drug he was taking. He had required this amount of medication ever since a car accident many years earlier had left him partially paralyzed.

My client began to experience strange symptoms after several long-distance healing sessions. He eventually realized the reason for the new symptoms: Because of the healing work, he no longer needed so much painkilling medication and it was time to lower the dosages. As soon as he did this, the new symptoms disappeared and he felt better with less medication.

As far as I can tell, tuning energy to achieve a more harmonious vibration has the potential to help just about anything. The experience of tuning an instrument, an animal, a human, or the relationship between any of them, feels similar to me. The results of working on a violin can be heard instantly. The outcome of healings on sentient beings can also be immediately clear and obvious or may take a variable amount of time to manifest. Sometimes the energy is rejected and there is no healing at all. My job is to tune from a state of love and joy and to offer beauty of vibration in dimensions heard and unheard. Equally important is to recognize what is not my job.

CHAPTER XII

Connecting the Dots

We appear to have the boundary of our skin to separate "our" physical body from the physical bodies of "others," and from objects around us. We also know that we can be deeply affected by people, animals, and events in ways that do not require physical touch. This very powerful effect that we have on each other is through the emotions.

A friend or family member having a good day may help you to have a better one. Associating with someone who is having a day that causes him or her to loudly wish that they had stayed in bed, or under it, may affect your *Happy Days Are Here Again* mood. An adult's reaction to the tears of a frightened child will likely determine whether the little one is comforted or not. Frazzled parents who ignore or yell at their sobbing offspring are not going to create a sense of peace and calm. Our emotions can have great impact on another's sense of happiness, well-being, and ultimately physical health.

I work in dimensions of healing energy where there is no difference between physical and emotional vibration. It is all silent sound. If frequencies feel to me as if they are not flowing in a person's acoustical field, it may be an emotional situation, or it may have already evolved into a physical one. The difficulty is not the emotion itself: it is the holding of the emotion that blocks the natural flow of energy. Swallowed anger, buried grief, and refusal to forgive are all vibrations, which, over time, manifest in our own bodies and can also affect the beings around us. In addition, anger, grief, fear, joy, and love make an imprint on physical objects. This is because *all is energy; energy expands; and energy affects energy.* And as long as we are talking about the secrets of the universe, *like attracts like.*

I didn't want to believe that the energy field of the musician had a particularly big effect on the instrument I was adjusting. I thought that would complicate the picture. I wanted to continue to believe that the violins were separate objects, which could always be tuned without considering the state of the humans who were playing them. Perhaps if I didn't look into the matter it would go away. *Wrong, Deena.*

Telling string players to get psychological therapy in order to stop messing up the sound of their instruments was not an appealing thought. It could soon leave a violin maker in search of a new career. This seemed to be even worse thinking than those violin makers who only pretended to move the soundpost because they assumed that most musicians were slightly crazed characters who wouldn't know the difference. The nagging thought remained: if I could deliberately change sound with telepathy, might the musicians be affecting their instruments inadvertently? Perhaps the unintentional influence of a player on his or her instrument was not as fast-acting as my purposeful energy sound adjustments, but a factor nevertheless.

It is no secret that a tense musician doesn't sound as good as a relaxed one—there is nothing metaphysical about that. The muscles of a stressed player become tighter and alter the way an instrument vibrates; the wood does not move as freely and the result is audible. However, I was beginning to suspect that the reasons for compromised instrument sound transcended physical explanations. Long before I had any thoughts about studying energy healing, I used to notice that just prior to auditions, the instruments of many string players became unpleasant and edgy. Violins that had been sounding well and playing easily for long periods of time suddenly became uncooperative.

After I began using mental energy for the purpose of acoustic adjustment, I was usually able to coax the violins (I am also referring to violas and cellos when I mention violins) into producing beautiful sound. However, there were notable exceptions where the sound did not improve no matter what I tried—physical or telepathic. Finally, with other options eliminated, all that was left for me to work with was the musician. The first several times I tried this the players were not present. I tuned into the musician's energy field and worked long distance. The results amazed me. In each case, the energy logjam was broken, and I was able to adjust the sound of the instrument much more easily.

After that, whenever I had a problem with an instrument, I worked with the energy field of its player. Sometimes after an instrument had been successfully adjusted, the beautiful sound would disappear in a couple of days or a couple of weeks. Out of desperation, I applied the same principles that I had learned for tuning difficult instruments—I began to work with the energy fields of the players. Frequently, a session or two of working on the energy fields of both the instrument and the musician solved the problem.

It is possible to perform a healing on a human only to have his or her energy field quickly shift out of harmony again, but usually, instruments played by clients who have had recent healing work are easier to tune and remain sounding lovely for a longer period of time. It certainly seemed as if humans and musical instruments had fields that were intertwined and interactive.

Eventually, I realized that it was *always* better to perform energy-tuning work on an instrument *and* its player. For best results, I now tune the musician and the instrument individually, as separate energy fields, and then together to harmonize the vibrations between them and create one cohesive energy unit.

The task of explaining to my clients that their thoughts and state of being may be affecting their instrument's sound and feel has been challenging. It seems as if I am blaming the players for all the acoustical troubles of their expensive wooden boxes. Those people who have stable instruments, even though their personal lives are disasters, merely add to the impression that I have gone quite mad. (If I ever figure out why some players can be emotional wrecks and not affect their instruments, I should try to bottle it.)

Over the years I have worked with Roberta Crawford, she has become very aware of her psychic influence on her instrument and bow. We experimented together; I tuned her (and not her viola) a little bit at a time and then we listened to her instrument after each quick adjustment on her energy field. The sound of the viola improved as Roberta's energy field improved. These days if her viola starts sounding poorly, she calls me for a healing on herself, first.

For the best results, we still work with the instrument's field as well as Roberta's field, but we learned from our observations that working on the player alone improves the sound of the instrument itself, even when tested by another musician. It is as if the musical instrument becomes an energetic extension of the player, like having another arm and hand. I asked Roberta to write up her perspective for this book, and she sent me the following:

Although I had known Bob and Deena Spear for years, it wasn't until 1985, when I brought my viola in for work to their shop in Alexandria, Virginia, that acquaintance deep-

ened into profound friendship and regard. I had little idea then how much my contact with Deena would impact my approach to viola playing, teaching, and most importantly, the art of living. Fifteen years and two violas (made by Bob and set up by Deena) later, it is astonishing to reflect back. So much of the transformation I have experienced musically and personally had its beginnings in our initial meetings that year.

I have worked closely with Deena since that time, at first traveling frequently to get adjustments on my instruments. Deena was relentless in her quest for a beautiful, balanced sound—and always experimenting. I was frequently on the spot when a new idea had just burst to the surface, requiring a human and instrumental guinea pig. It was in turns exciting, exhilarating, exasperating, and hilarious.

My violas graciously endured applications of bits of clay and tiny blocks of wood at key spots, as Deena sought to balance the vibrating body of wood with the air mass (mode matching). I became adept at sidestepping queries from colleagues with vague murmurs about acoustic experimentation. The fact is I couldn't possibly explain what Deena was doing, I just knew it worked. I watched Deena remove infinitesimal scrapings of wood from various parts of the viola using tools that appeared to have been lifted from a "Star Wars" set. I looked on as my viola was gently strapped into a harness to have its vibrational signature measured. We worked into the wee hours as Deena adjusted first one component, then another in her continuous search for the perfect sound. The results were always marvelous. My viola sounded and felt wonderful. It was a joy to play.

But inevitably, there would come a time following the adjustment, when things would go sour. Beauty and ease would gradually diminish to be replaced by increasing tension and effort. At these points I would often feel anxiety, anger, and despair.

Over time, as Deena's research became increasingly more subtle and she focused on healing sound with energy, she began to discover the critical connection between the physical/emotional state of the player and the vibrational well-being of the viola. It became clear that viola, bow, and player function as an energy unit. If the player is experiencing disharmony in his/her energy field, it will directly impact the equipment.

I have had countless experiences, which have led (really forced!) me to accept this connection. For several years I experienced a series of incidents with bows that I had loved suddenly ceasing to sound, feel, or even work right in the most basic ways. The more I reacted negatively to the situation, the more impossible it became to use the bow in question. For a while, it seemed I was continuously bow shopping. Fate finally intervened. Potential financial disaster and exhaustion from the continuous search thankfully coupled with Deena's advice led me toward a new attitude. Her energy healing work with me and my bows helped to correct the problem and the need for new bows.

I also recall an adjustment Deena did for me on my viola just prior to an important performance. She helped my instrument to sound fantastic. It was thrilling! However, as I continued to play, I discovered, I couldn't find a way to "feel" balanced with my viola. No matter what I did the viola felt clumsy and I felt out of control, out of "sync" with it. For me that concert was a nightmare, although people told me I sounded fine. In speaking with Deena afterwards, we realized that while she had tuned the viola, she hadn't checked my energy field. After this experience we always check in to see how I'm doing when adjusting the viola.

This has led to some fascinating experiences, and to the conclusion that, at least in my case, the disharmony I experience with my viola always has its roots in a disharmony within myself. If I address this first, my viola, even if not in tiptop condition, can sound acceptable.

Over the years our adjustment sessions have increasingly taken place long distance. That is, Deena adjusts me and the viola over the phone. The results are as amazing as our in-person sessions, and have provided many opportunities for spontaneous experimentation. My acceptance of this subtle work has occurred over time and I have come to trust that Deena's wildest, most way-out theories deserve careful attention. As time has passed, I've begun to apply the idea of conceiving inner joy and beauty as a means of transforming sound for myself. I've also applied it to the kinesthetic motions involved in playing and energetic harmony between individuals in the teaching studio. The energy work has also gradually led me to believe that we have the potential to enhance our everyday world through our thinking and that this power is available to all of us at all moments of our lives. It's just a thought away!

Roberta Crawford, Violist
Music faculty, Binghamton University, Binghamton, New York
Associate Director, Finger Lakes Chamber Ensemble

I have been known to admit that there are physical factors such as weather or open seams that affect musical instrument sound, so I don't dare blame (I mean lovingly accuse) the musician's emotional state for every instance of an instrument's crankiness—just most of them. It's not always clear who got out-of-sorts first, but usually both parties can use a boost to create the most beautiful music:

I remember when you and Bob were at the temple when Steck had a chamber concert. Bob's cello, which I love, was feeling a little grumpy that day. That made me a little grumpy, but you came over and offered to help. After making sure we were unobserved, I said, "Go for it." You passed yours hands over the cello and suddenly the responsiveness and my disposition were restored. Halleluiah! My wife said later that it sounded (for a change) like I had been practicing.

John Martin
Principal Cellist, National Symphony Orchestra 1948–1994

Chapter XIII

The Letters of the Hebrew Alphabet

*E*very energy healing, whether on a musical instrument, human, or animal, is an adventure and a learning experience for me. One healing was particularly memorable. My client was Roberta Herzog, who works professionally as an intuitive to help people resolve problems by giving them knowledge about other lifetimes, which are relevant to their current difficulty. She specializes in obtaining this information and is very good at it. But on that day she was supposed to be *my* client.

We were scarcely two minutes into our long-distance phone session when she said to me, "I don't do friends and family. I'm not that kind of medium, but there is someone here who is a male ancestor on your father's side. He was a famous Rabbi and a Kabbalist and he wants you to begin to work with the letters of the Hebrew alphabet." I knew that I had a famous Rabbi on my father's side of the family who was my great-great-grandfather, although I did not know he was a Kabbalist. Kabbalists are those who study and use the Kabbala, the Ancient Jewish Mystery Teachings.

Although I had gone to Hebrew school as a child and could still vaguely remember the letters of the Hebrew alphabet, we had not learned anything about the Kabbala. The topic was considered too esoteric for children and I doubt my teachers were interested in it themselves. Even as I became an adult I never studied anything about the subject and to some extent lost touch with my Jewish heritage. This was about to change.

I asked if the man were Joel Zalkind, and he said that he was. Rabbi Joel Zalkind, although my great-great-grandfather, was no ordinary family member. He had such a presence that Roberta agreed to continue receiving instructions for me. I was to make up a deck of the letters of the Hebrew alphabet. Index cards were recommended for this purpose. It was suggested that I hold the cards face down and simply pick the one that felt appropriate for the healing, without seeing which letter I was choosing. Once I had made my selection, I was to then turn over the card and look at the letter. I was told that the shapes and the sounds of the letters themselves had powerful multidimensional vibrations and that as I learned to work with them, my healings would increase in speed and depth. Of course, I didn't have to do any of this, but there was much potential here. This communication relayed, we returned to the healing that I was supposed to be doing on Roberta.

The circuits in my brain became scrambled. Lights began to flash at random. Silent alarms begged "Security" to return from lunch and man their battle stations. . . . It was too late. I was already quite sure that Roberta had received a genuine communication for me from my great-great-grandfather. Not everyone has a famous Rabbi on their father's side, and she was hardly looking to act as a conduit for one of my dead relatives. The session was supposed to be a healing for her. However, those in spirit who want to get a message through to my physical plane consciousness have to pick their moments when they have the chance. Roberta had the telepathic gifts and the Rabbi saw his opportunity.

Whatever was or wasn't involved in the vibrations of the letters, I was not convinced that I could make use of them. Dubious and resistant, I let the ideas percolate for over a week. (It must be annoying to be an evolved spirit who bothers to find a way to get an important message through to some clueless mortal who then sits around doing nothing but panic instead of just trying the suggestion.) When my neural search parties failed to track down a good reason not to make the Hebrew alphabet deck, I finally collected the materials and created the cards.

What was I supposed to do now? I felt insecure and incompetent. I chose a letter and looked at it. I silently spoke the letter name. It felt a little vague, but I did sense a vibration. Finally, my teeth stopped chattering. I grabbed another letter. Even with the dental clatter I could tell that it gave me a different sensation from the first one. Small puffs of smoke arose from distant areas inside my head. I pressed on.

I began to choose letters for healings with the cards face down so I would not see which letter attracted me until after I had made the selection. Curious things happened. For example, I had several situations with clients that involved the mouth or throat. Each time, without looking at the cards, I picked the Hebrew letter "Pey." There were other letters that seemed to be chosen repeatedly for other themes. A couple of times I even returned the cards to the deck and reshuffled, but chose the very same letter again, without consciously knowing which one I was selecting. Now, this was getting spooky.

Eventually, I rustled up the nerve to try the letters when tuning instruments. Because the musicians and I could immediately hear the results, if any, this took more courage than using the Hebrew alphabet during human healings. The first several sessions were long-distance ones, over the phone. I felt I would be calmer and less attached to the outcome this way. The tunings seemed to go more quickly using the vibrations of the letters, and the changes in sound had a new flavor to them, according to the musicians who were helping me. I was in favor of anything that made the tuning process faster and easier. It was time to replace the obsolete alarm system and rewire my brain.

My intuitive friend, Louise Cook, obtained additional guidance for me. It was suggested that I not read anything about Kabbala for an unspecified time, so as not to be influenced by anyone else's ideas, which might not be correct for me. For the moment, it was best to observe what was happening and to get to know how to use the letters in my own unique way. I experimented for a number of weeks and then finally purchased some reading material on the subject of the Kabbala. One important book I bought was *The Book of Letters: A Mystical Alef-bait* by Lawrence Kushner. I was stunned to see that the Hebrew word, pronounced almost the same (peh) as the letter name "pey," meant mouth. This letter symbolized the mouth. Although I had noticed themes for other letters in my healings, they didn't necessarily align with the ones I was reading about in my newly acquired literature, but "pey" certainly did.

Roberta Herzog later told me that what I am doing is not really Kabbala, and that I am using the letters in a new way, not known in our current day. Also, because the letters are multidimensional, there is much more to each one than a few pages written in a book.

I began to have sessions with Roberta to obtain information on the meaning of the letters for me in my healing practice. Roberta has studied Kabbala herself, and the information that came through seemed to be a mix of traditional and nontraditional meanings for the letters. I continued to observe which letters I blindly chose for the healings on sentient beings and musical instruments.

Then Marlene Sandler said that she would be interested to see what information she could receive for each letter. She had no background in the Hebrew alphabet or the Kabbala—a similar situation to our beginnings with violins, which initially earned her Guarneri's query as to why I had a "fool for a channel." It was interesting to note where the information from the two independent intuitives overlapped, and where I was given seemingly different aspects of the letters. In addition to all of this channeled information, I had my observations as to which letters were chosen for various healing themes.

I used the deck and the letters consciously for quite some time. Eventually, I believe the letters began to automatically incorporate into the healings without my conscious participation. Initially, following the protocol with the index cards had introduced me to the amazing vibrations of these energies, and I became convinced of their power, which I'm sure I still barely tap into. (It is said that they are connected with the vibrations of creation.)

I asked Philip Pan, Concertmaster of the Jacksonville Symphony Orchestra for his impressions of the tunings when I began consciously using the Hebrew letters. He was very familiar with my instrument energy work, both in person and long distance, before this new addition. He sent me the following for this book:

> *The speed and accuracy of Deena's adjustments had been improving steadily over time, but the Hebrew letters seemed to bring a new and unique factor to the process—the factor of tonal character. Just as the tenor of Placido Domingo can easily be distinguished from that of Luciano Pavoratti, so can the voice of one violin be discerned from another. With the great string instruments, this distinction can best be described as an individual character or personality, and every single instrument, including those from the same master maker, has its own unmistakable personality just as every human being on earth does.*
>
> *The first time Deena used a Hebrew letter to work on my Bernandel's sound, I was only concerned with the fiddle's playability; I was not requesting any changes in its character. But I got more than I asked for. Besides improving in response and depth, the instrument took on a new voice. It was not completely divorced from the qualities I had come to love and expect from it, but there was a distinct transformation, much like the evolution of a promising vocal talent into mature artistry. Needless to say, this was great fun for me as I learned to make use of these new tonal dimensions.*

Our second experience with a Hebrew letter was even more dramatic. I would describe the basic character of my violin as very dark and rather serious, sort of an "old man" quality. Well, this time, the old man got a drink from the Fountain of Youth! The entire range of the instrument acquired a sparkle and zip that I can best describe as a person who has emerged from an arduous spiritual journey to discover newfound joy and enthusiasm for life. It is still tonally a very "dark" or baritone violin, but it now possesses a complex mix of over-tones on top of the deep bass foundation. The new tone colors are undoubtedly measurable on appropriate electronic devices. Interestingly, the letter Deena chose for this tuning is itself char-acterized by happiness, and I have recently been seeking to produce a more joyous expression in my playing. Mere coincidence? Ask me again after the next tuning. . . .

CHAPTER XIV

Voiceovers

The nice thing about tuning violins is that I instantly know what is happening. If there is not enough bass, mid-range, high-range, depth, focus, or power, I have only to listen with physical ears in order to discover the problem. As I gained more skill, I learned to detect many of these factors using my inner senses in the silent sound of the energy, but sometimes by listening with physical hearing, I noticed glitches that I had missed with my intuitive radar. For several years I wished that I had such an obvious diagnostic for my human clients as I did for the instruments.

One day a client asked me if she could bring her guitar to our in-person healing session. (She lived in Southern Maryland and didn't need to cross The Woodrow Wilson Bridge to come to my house.) She requested that I tune her guitar, which she played while singing to her four-year-old child at bedtime. As she began to demonstrate her musical good-night, I realized that I could probably do at least as much for her voice as I could for her guitar. That suited her fine, so I improved the sound of her guitar, her silent energy field, and her audible singing voice.

It was then that I realized that people's speaking and singing voices hold a lot of clues about how their bodies are vibrating. Listening to a violin is not only hearing the string (which is set into oscillation from the friction of a moving bow), but also the movement of the entire wooden box and surrounding air. Likewise, listening to the human voice reflects the vibration of the whole body, not just the larynx.

I began to pay more attention to human voices. To me, each human voice is a kind of string orchestra. Using that analogy, people who are stressed and ungrounded seem to have voices whose relative frequencies and harmonics are mostly in the violin range, with maybe a few violas tossed in for sanity. I discovered that by doing energy tunings, I could bring back missing frequency ranges as well as resonance into the speaking and singing voice, so it sounds to me like all the musicians in the orchestra have returned to their seats and begun to play.

To tune the voice, I sing individual notes and ask my clients to repeat the notes back to me, regardless of whether they think they can sing or not. The results have been fascinating. Sometimes a person simply could not hear the pitch of the note I was singing, and they sang everything but that note back to me. When I checked his or her energy field, that frequency was stuck, indicating physical or emotional problems connected with that vibrational range. I discovered that the tuning work would free the frequency, and then the person could hear me and sing the note back correctly. I found it was easiest to do a silent healing first to get the general energy flowing better, and then listen to the voice note by note in order to fine-tune the healing.

When working with trained or professional singers there is not as obvious a diagnostic indicator as the inability to repeat a note back to me, but the array of harmonics in each note often still tells me where to adjust acoustics for physical or emotional problems. I channel energy to heal the compromised frequencies in a manner similar to energy adjusting violins.

When I have performed voice-tuning sessions on non-singers and even people who considered themselves to be tone deaf, so far I have been able to get each person to the point where he or she can sing the correct note back to me. I had one client who told me she had never been able to sing the note A for her entire life. I performed a two-hour silent healing, and then a voice-tuning. After that, singing an A was as easy for her as watching someone else vacuum my house is for me.

Sometimes a happy side-effect of tuning someone's energy field and voice has been an improvement in the ability to play a musical instrument. I asked Grace Ackerman to describe her experience with our long-distance healing sessions:

> *I ran into Deena through a friend who had done a tuning session and found her cello playing much improved, even though she hadn't practiced at all between lessons. The improvement was significant enough that even her teacher commented on it. Well, I'm a beginning guitar student, came to it very late in life (57) and was/am eager to absorb all I can about*

music as fast as possible. I had a handicap, in that my motor development was inhibited due to some problems I experienced as a baby. I am slow in things that require great coordination and small, precise hand motions. Once I started to play of course, I ran into this one head on. My teacher is patient, but I could see he felt bad for me when I had to struggle so much for each new skill. So, when I heard of Deena from my friend, I e-mailed her to set up a session.

I should mention that although I do believe that 'extra-physical' interaction is possible, it has been my experience that there are a lot more people indulging in wishful thinking than are actually engaging in healing and other kinds of energy work. I'm an honest skeptic, that is, I really check things out before I'm willing to believe that something psychic or extra-physical actually happened. I need proof. That proof can be in the form of testimony from other people whose judgment I trust, or it can be from my own personal experience, which is the best as far as I'm concerned.

The first session, and the several others I've had since, are simple to describe on a physical level. Deena had me count from one to five, then she'd work for a bit and then we'd do it again. The first session I couldn't feel what was going on, but did notice changes in the clarity and resonance of my voice as we proceeded from counting to singing one note at a time. I was lying on my back as we did the tuning, a position which never produces good vocal tone for me, but that too improved during the course of the session.

Deena said she felt a lot of anger and sorrow, both of which I know are there in abundance due to some serious problems early in my life. It's a subject I had decided never to deal with since I felt I couldn't handle the raw emotion involved in doing so, but now that I need to get by those barriers in order to play, I have to do what I thought was impossible and look the old stuff in the eye, so to speak.

At the end of the first session, I felt that something had happened, but couldn't put my finger on it. It wasn't until the next morning that the truck hit. When I woke up, I was so exhausted I could barely drag myself out of bed. At first I thought I was ill, but then I realized what it was and why Deena had advised me to do it on a night when I didn't have to get up the next day. (I had thought it was just because I was up a bit past my bedtime.) When I exercise a lot either physically or psychically after a long period of abstinence, I feel the effects, and boy, did I. I could tell there was some serious integration going on after though, so I wasn't particularly worried.

The next day I was fine, and much more relaxed at my lesson; also, I noticed that I had reclaimed a few notes in my lower vocal range, something I hadn't been able to do since taking singing lessons over 40 years ago.

The several sessions I've had with Deena have resulted in gradual improvement in my voice, and, I believe (although this is harder to 'prove'), my ability to change chords quickly on my guitar. The whole first year I took lessons I felt as if my progress were minuscule, but now the learning is coming faster. I'm practicing hard of course, but I practiced hard the first year too and I didn't get very far. I believe some of this improvement is due to the sessions, which basically help to remove obstacles I've set in my own way, as all of us do. One additional benefit I've found from these sessions is that, with each session, my ability to monitor and work with my own energies has improved. I'm kind of learning as I go.

The most recent session I had was focused on tuning my favorite Taylor 512 guitar to me and vice versa. This session was unique in that it was easier to hear the changes in the sound of my instrument as Deena worked, and I was also able to feel what was happening with the energy far more clearly than in previous sessions. It resulted in an increase of depth and richness in the sound of the guitar so that one of my teachers has hardly been able to keep his hands off it since. He keeps remarking what a big sound it has for its size. And, yes, it does—now.

So, in my opinion, the tuning work Deena does has been a great help to me in getting where I want to go musically, and has been fun and instructive as well. As my instrument collection expands, I will set up future sessions so that each one can be uniquely mine.

Grace Ackerman, August 9, 1999

I consider voice tuning to be an important addition to an energy detox session. Even though the silent healing usually succeeds in changing toxic substances into something more harmonious (benign), the voice can show me places where the body is still affected, and helps to guide me to areas of frequency that can use further fine-tuning. I don't necessarily need to know that a particular organ or other part of the body is in difficulty, because when I channel the energy to fix the acoustical disharmony, it repairs or contributes to the repair of the physical (or emotional) problem "automagically."

Trying to analyze the situation can get in the way of innocently acting as a bridge for the energy. I have simply observed physical and emotional benefit from tuning voices. This does not mean that a professional singer is healthier than a tone-deaf person. I use a different standard for the diagnostic in each case.

An interesting thing I noticed was that if I merged my energy field with the field of a human client, the harmonic structure of the notes I sang became similar to that of my client. In the past I have used this curious phenomenon when working with animals, since I could not ask them to speak or sing, nor do many dogs, cats, or horses use the phone—a primitive device for communication far inferior to the telepathy possessed by the animals. Furthermore, I imagine they can't figure out the long-distance rates any better than I can. So I occasionally sang notes aloud while merged with the animal's field, just to get extra information to locate blocked frequencies. I think it was one of those things best done in private.

CHAPTER XV

Truth in Advertising

I hope there will come a day when the idea and practice of energy healing will be as commonplace as McDonalds and Pizza Hut are now. At present, many people who come to a healer do so as a last resort. A number of clients who are referred to me for health problems are rather skeptical at first. It is difficult to be otherwise given the prevailing popular beliefs and media exposure. Because much of my practice was and is long distance, this presents an even greater mental leap for some of my clients who are new to energy work. Many of these first time recipients can accept the idea that healing energy might work, but only if I am right in the room with them, my hands touching or just above their bodies.

Nothing about the way we perceive physical reality, with our "usual" physical senses—the ones deemed "real" by society—prepares us to imagine how I, or any other healer, could touch into and affect the field of someone hundreds or thousands of miles away. I believe that, as the decades go by, this will change. Just as some of the great artists and composers were given scathing reviews in their day, I believe that those blazing the trail in the prevention and treatment of illness at the source will eventually be known, accepted, appreciated, and utilized by the majority of the population. It could be a long wait. By then, probably someone will be channeling me—unless, inexplicably, I become well-known, in which case 50 people will be claiming to channel me.

I belong to a worldwide network of healers through the Internet where a recent hot topic of discussion was Diane Goldner's book, *Infinite Grace,* which is about healing and various healing schools. Some had strong criticisms of the book, others generally liked it, and some were most enthusiastic. I bought a copy and read it. I then sent it on to friend and colleague Carol Kulig, who graduated from Brennan Healing Science Training two years ahead of me, and who also works professionally as a healer. After reading part of the Goldner book, she e-mailed me a message, which practically had me rolling on the floor with laughter. I think it deserves a wider readership, so I will include it here. Perhaps that doesn't exactly guarantee her a bestseller size audience—at least not right now. (My friend Marianne assures me that my book will be well respected in 200 years.) Anyway, here are Carol's comments:

> *We certainly do need a few good background books about healing and energy work. I wonder how much of a readership the Goldner book will actually have. Won't it be a relief when what we do is more generally known, so that we don't have to start explaining from before square one with practically every client?*
>
> *What if M.D.'s practices were generally unknown? Can you imagine the conversation where a doctor recommends surgery: Well, we all dress up in white, put on masks, and go into a special room. You are lying down there under a bright light without any clothes on. I cut your body open with a very sharp knife and we all look inside. You bleed a lot but a masked woman sucks up the blood with a little vacuum cleaner. I rearrange your insides the way I think they ought to be and take out any I don't think are really necessary. Then I sew your skin up with a needle and thread and go home. It hurts a lot and some people die right then and there.*
>
> *That would be a pretty hard sell without all the advance PR work the medical profession has behind it. Don't you think?*

CHAPTER XVI

A New Chapter

No more Woodrow Wilson Bridge. It's still there with its increasing moments of infamous gridlock, but I'm not. I am now writing from my new home in Ithaca, New York where I have joined my husband, who has been building our house and future healing center for a couple of years. I wrote the previous chapters more than a year and a half ago as there has been little time, until now, to complete this book.

Several months after my move from Maryland to New York, my mother was diagnosed with cancer. She decided that at the age of nearly 86 she was finished with whatever she wanted to do with her life and, believing she could not be helped, opted for no treatment of any kind. While she didn't verbally turn down healing work, none was accepted on an energy level. This was not surprising since she no longer had any interest in being here. She made her transition eight months after I left Maryland.

My mother was like a force of nature. If she labeled a particular direction North, then it *was* North as far as anyone in her vicinity was concerned. The fact that the rest of the world believed her chosen North to be East was not relevant.

If the Kennedy Center barricades were positioned to block the entrance of vehicles because the parking garage was full, and if my mother thought she should be permitted to park there anyway, the barricades were temporarily moved aside and she drove into the garage and found a place to park. I still can't imagine what she said to the attendants. My husband, Bob, and I were in our own car following behind her and were turned away like all the other mortals who had to go park some eight blocks distant.

If an item from a store were non-returnable, it became returnable when my mother appeared with it. Once, when a store didn't see it her way, she took them to court—over a robe. She won of course, with the judge's compliments.

The events I described took place when my mother was in her 80s. Another memorable episode, which also occurred during those same years, was the time my mother went to a sale, but took such a hard fall on some uneven pavement that she had to go to the emergency room for treatment. Damaged, but undeterred, she left the hospital. When she did not return home, family members became concerned. Eventually she resurfaced and told her astonished family where she had been. "I went back to the store," she said, "The sale wasn't over."

My father has been very close to me since he left his physical body. My mother, after eight months of absence from the physical plane, has so far not been a presence here. I think that many people who die are delighted to discover that they are not dead. I believe my father was one of those. I'm not so sure this was the case for my mother. I have heard from her just once through an intuitive and it was very brief. She never believed in mediums anyway. I understand from those who have seen her in the dimension in which she is now focused, that she is supposed to be going to class and is not thrilled about it.

Some years ago, when both my parents were still alive (in the physical plane) my father would say of my mother, that if she didn't want something a certain way, "God wouldn't dare." Few crossed my mother here on earth. God has eternity on his side.

In life, my mother's sense of logic made it difficult for her to see how I could possibly do what I claimed to do. She also knew me to be truthful, and she was aware that high-level musicians were bringing their instruments to me for acoustical adjustments even after I no longer used physical tools for that purpose. She supported my work, despite the fact that it made no sense to her. I am grateful for this. By the time we are once again face-to-face, perhaps she will have been to more classes, and I won't seem like such an odd duck to her. (Or perhaps I will have realized that I am an odd duck.)

My healing practice is the one constant that I have had since my move. I have continued to perform most healings long distance, except for working in person on a few musical instruments. Shortly after my arrival in New York, it became obvious that I was going to have to make a major change in the way I was working. The problem had nothing to do with whether or not I saw a client in person, but rather how I handled the energy. Most of the recipients of my work were experiencing healing from the energy I channeled and they were just fine, but my own teeth were not. I managed to vibrate every last one of them loose by running the energy through my mouth.

I did succeed in using energy to glue all but one tooth back in. This tooth was of course next to my front teeth in plain view for all to see. I felt that all I needed to do was to have that tooth removed and then go around smiling and saying to people (small children in particular) "and how are you, my pretty?" (A pointy black hat would also have added a nice touch.) If I didn't already have a very strange reputation, that should have done it.

The tooth, which I was unable to heal, had already been compromised for years for reasons other than overdosing it with too many vibrations. It had been entirely without bone well before I had even contemplated any professions not listed in my junior high school's career aptitude test. I think it remained in my mouth merely out of habit. I struggled for months to save the tooth, but to no avail. It is very much more difficult to heal oneself, both because it is so hard to detach from one's own energy field and because it is much easier to love everybody else.

I had a consolation prize. By the time I went to the dentist to have the poor tooth extracted, I was able to perform a detox *on myself,* prior to the Carbocain injection, so there were no side effects from the chemical and no need to clear it from my body afterward. More than eight years of healing work, and I finally managed to do something meaningful on myself.

The particular technique I used in order to detox ahead of time, I call the "chemo-cloud." It represented a big advance for me, not just because I was able to achieve results on myself, but also because I was able to successfully perform it at all on anyone. In the past I had always waited 24 hours and then sent healing energy to clear toxic side effects in a chemotherapy patient's body. But if I delayed the clearing until after the infusion of chemicals, there were already unwanted side effects and the energy detoxing procedure became more difficult, more time consuming, and possibly less complete. However, that process was my guidance at the time, and it fit the abilities I had then. Thus my protocol for several years was to give the chemicals the opportunity to accomplish the job for which they were intended, even though the delay might allow some damage to occur that I might not be able to reverse.

By the time Linda Y. came along, my boxes weren't unpacked from the move, but my healing work had advanced considerably, thanks to the lessons learned from the episode with my teeth. I was doing much more with pure thought, rather than running energy through my body—and mouth. When Nancy hired me to work with her sister, Linda, I obtained intuitive readings with several practitioners. They all said the same thing—she was not planning to survive her illness. The cancer was too widespread. The unhappiness that was the root cause of the illness was so deep that it was more than she thought she could heal during this life.

I shared this information with Nancy, but not with Linda herself. My job was to help Linda stay comfortable, help her deal with fear, and ultimately help her with the transition from the physical body to spirit. (It takes energy to die. Having additional energy available that can be used for this purpose—if it is needed and desired by the person receiving the energy—is part of healing work.)

Linda had surgery just before I became involved with her case. The doctors had originally intended to remove some of the tumors, but when they saw the great extent of the cancer, they chose to simply close up the incision and not remove anything. Instead, a decision was made to give Linda chemotherapy, even though I don't think the doctors expected to save her life.

My guide was not amused. Linda's sister, Nancy, called me just as the medical personnel were starting to drip the first chemo into Linda, who lives hundreds of miles from me. Fortunately, I was scheduled to talk to my friend Louise Cook about two minutes after Nancy phoned me. Louise, who has just turned 80, sees and hears people's angel guides. She discovered this gift in her mid 60s.

I called Louise with my agenda for our conversation now rearranged. I told her about the just-beginning chemotherapy and asked for her assistance in obtaining information. Louise tuned in telepathically and conveyed my guide's communication to me. He said the chemo would be extremely jarring for Linda and that there was nothing at all positive about this medical therapy in her case. He described how I could make a kind of energy cloud around her that would be infused along with the chemicals as they entered her body. He commented that Linda would likely choose to use this energy cloud to nullify the effects of the chemo completely.

He added later that in other cases, people might choose to utilize some of the chemical if it served a purpose for them. As always, the choice of how to use the energy is up to the recipient. Louise, continuing to translate, said that the cloud technique, which she had just described, works best if created as close to the onset of the chemical infusion as possible. I was nervous but made the protective cloud right then while we were still on the phone. I was surprised when it took less than a minute, but Louise, listening to my guide, verified that it had been created properly.

The doctors continued the chemotherapy treatment with Linda almost every week for many months, and I continued to make the "chemocloud" before each session. Linda never felt nauseated and never lost her hair. She had no side effects. The doctors were baffled. Although using thought had considerably sped up my work, I was absolutely amazed that a healing technique performed so quickly and easily was so powerful.

As I am typing this, Linda is still alive in her physical body. She is tired, but comfortable, and is just now beginning to show signs of the fluid build-up, which usually means that cancer is advancing, although her oncologist says the recent CAT scan shows that a tumor on the pancreas is no longer visible and cancer markers in the blood have dropped from 1.5 million to 39 thousand. Despite the mixed signals, I feel the original "read" that Linda is not planning to stay is likely still correct, but I can't be certain this is the case.

Fortunately, I don't need to know in order to send healing, as she will use the energy according to her own decisions. So far she has used it to stay pain-free, and I hope this continues. I am very grateful to have the ability to be of service when medical choices are being made that are not in harmony with one's being. I watched this happen with my father, but I was not advanced enough in my work at that time to help him.

I am also grateful to Louise for bringing much other information that has made such a difference in this case, in my life and in the lives of others. I am now being told that soon I will have to trust myself, and that others will not be able to bring in the information for me because it will be initially unique to me and new to this dimension and cannot be clearly received through other channels. So much has been gained from the intuitive help of others. I've considered myself a good conduit for energy, but not information, so this is a little scary—like driving on the D.C. beltway (toward The Woodrow Wilson Bridge) during summer rush hour, without an oxygen mask.

CHAPTER XVII

A Salt Cure

I often refer my clients to those who can offer additional support. It may be to an intuitive like Marlene, Louise, or Carla, in order to learn about issues underlying their illnesses, which are not being addressed, or to a homeopathic physician, or to someone who specializes in nutrition (especially if a client may have a severely compromised digestive system, which could require supplements and/or a change in diet). Sometimes I refer people to Roberta Herzog to look at a past life situation (although technically, as I understand it, all lives are actually simultaneous and it is really a matter of focus. Jane Roberts' book, *Seth Speaks*, is very helpful on this topic, as is *The Infinite Mind* by Valerie Hunt).

In the following case, Roberta Herzog referred Linda N. to me when my name surfaced during their session as someone who could help. No rogue past lives, which would have shed light on the cause of the problem, had shown up in Roberta's reading. Nor was there any further information as to why the referral was to me in particular.

Linda N. called me and explained that her preteen son had multiple problems that his physicians had labeled as everything from attention deficit disorder to mild autism, but really, the doctors seemed clueless. Her son had problems in school and at home, which included lack of focus and emotional outbursts. There were also symptoms of something like seizures, although not exactly full-blown. This was a bright child, but definitely out of sync with himself and the world. Medication was not resolving the problem; in fact, it was making it worse.

About 10 minutes into our first phone conversation, Linda "happened" to mention that their family dog, now deceased, had also developed neurological problems. Something struck me (probably one of my guides giving me a whack with his megaphone lest I not hear him for a change) when she mentioned her dog. Two sentient beings in the same household both showing neurological problems did not sound like coincidence to me. I immediately suspected a common cause.

I had worked with several animals and humans who had been exposed to, and poisoned by, Dursban, a chemical pesticide that has just been banned. Among these clients was Gia Miele, who tells her story in Chapter X of this book. I thought I recognized the symptoms from previous experience (no offense to my long-sought psychic ability). I began to ask questions about the timing of the onset of physical or emotional difficulties both for the dog and for this child. It seemed as though problems began to arise years earlier, when Linda's family had first moved into their new old house. I asked if they had engaged an exterminator to come to spray for termites, knowing that the timing of their house purchase coincided with an era in which Dursban had been employed. Sure enough, the house, or at least the basement, had been treated just prior to their moving in. I later called their exterminator to confirm that Dursban was the product used. It was.

At the time of the pesticide application, Linda's son was a newborn baby, with a young sensitive system. Dursban is a neurotoxin. I felt that both the child and the dog had been affected. The youngster has been chemically sensitive most of his life. Whether this happened before or because of the Dursban I don't know, but I was now fairly confident that the original cause of the problems was neurological damage from the termite treatment. I also had an inkling as to why Linda was sent to me: I might recognize the cause of the symptoms, having dealt with them on several occasions before, as well as have some skills to help the situation.

I had concerns because Linda's call to me came many years after the initial chemical exposure. However, Gia's Dursban-induced seizures had been immediately halted even though my energy healing work had been performed four years after her exposure. I felt there was still much to be gained by doing a clearing and an energy tuning, but I didn't know what could be done for the chemicals that might still be emanating from the basement of the house, given the persistence of Dursban. "Oh, good," I thought, "These people live in an expensive house in a very well-to-do neighborhood and I'm going to suggest that they should move?" Perhaps a career manicuring alligator nails would be simpler.

Dursban replaced an equally awful chemical called Chlordane, which was so bad that someone in the government finally had the sense to ban it. Of course it's just a matter of time before whatever replaced Dursban is banned too, provided we have any sanity of environmental laws in place at all, and you can't bet your petroleum milkshake on that either. As I type this, our current president is busy weakening various standards (in order to make higher concentrations of toxins legal), such as the amount of arsenic allowed in drinking water. Just wait until the lead lobby hears about that; they'll be just green with envy, or maybe just green.

Perhaps for this publication our commander-in-chief and leader of the free world shall remain nameless, or some might say shameless. That of course would not be me as I strive to be non-judgmental. OK, so sometimes I fail. What do I know? Perhaps these guys believe we will all be saved by antimicrobial soap. (As spiritual penance I offer the nine P's: Practice Pity for the Poor Patriotic Politicians who Poison the Planet for Personal Profit. PPPPPPPPPth! That's a Bronx cheer for short.)

I called Louise. My suspicions about the termite treatment and the baby were confirmed. She also mentioned that much could be done with healing energy now to help the situation. She obtained information from my guide telling me how to remedy the situation, but the problem of residual pesticide in the house required additional measures.

The information Louise received for the latter problem involved getting pure camphor, the kind that is made from a particular tree and not the fake variety that is usually sold in drug stores today. The camphor could be in the form of chunks or oil. Rock salt, the sodium chloride material one puts in water softeners, was also needed. Fortunately, it was inexpensive and readily available. The final ingredient was energy, channeled by me (long distance in this case) to activate the salt/camphor mixture, which was then placed in each corner of the basement in open containers (such as pie plates or paper dishes). At the end of about a week, the material was to be taken up and transported straight to the dump because of the toxins it had absorbed. The procedure was to be repeated several times.

After speaking very briefly with the young man by phone to be sure that I was connected to his energy, I performed an hour-long healing on him. When I began, his energy field felt completely scattered and disorganized. At the end of the session his field felt to me to be centered and tuned, like a well-functioning musical instrument. Linda bought the camphor and rock salt and I energized the mixture. She followed the directions for putting out the ingredients and then bringing them to the dump after the appropriate number of days. Over several months, the salt and camphor procedure was repeated a few times.

Immediately following the hour-long energy healing, some improvements were noted in the boy. Other changes have been gradual, but steady. His behavior and his focus have so improved that he was able to leave the school for children with emotional disabilities and enter a special program to help him catch up on the schoolwork he has missed.

When I called Linda to read her this chapter, she mentioned that, in addition to the dog, there had been another member of the household who had developed neurological problems—her canary. She told me that at one point she had mentioned the canary to one of the doctors, but he was not interested in considering any environmental influences because that was "outside his area of expertise."

I hadn't remembered all the problems that had resulted from trying to resolve the initial chemical insult, which I believe to have been the Dursban. Linda graciously agreed to add more details and clarification in the hope that perhaps a parent or doctor reading this book may learn from her experience. I know that reviewing these events has been painful to her, and I am grateful to Linda for telling her story:

Even as a baby, my son showed signs of chemical sensitivity. At the age of three, he began to exhibit frequent emotional outbursts that resembled autism. At eight years old he had a particularly severe episode in the doctor's office. The intensity of the outburst caused the doctor, a pediatric psychiatrist, to prescribe a low dose of an antipsychotic drug.

Within a year and a half my son began having an involuntary tic, which consisted of tongue thrusting. The doctor switched him to a different antipsychotic. After beginning this new drug, my son developed a speech impediment—hesitation and stuttering when attempting to start sentences. The situation grew so bad that in desperation I once gave him pen and paper for communication and we considered sign language.

I tried repeatedly to explain to the doctor what was happening, but he was unable to consider that we were experiencing a drug reaction, as it didn't fit the profile. I communicated with a representative of the drug's manufacturer, but was also ignored. The excuse given was that it wasn't tested in children.

I was so concerned that we then went to a neurologist who gave my son an EEG that showed abnormal brain waves. It was suggestive of seizure, but he was not able to label it that completely, so he called it disorganized EEG. The neurologist prescribed an antiseizure medication. After beginning this drug, the speech problems increased.

Finally the pediatric psychologist noticed the problem and withdrew the antipsychotic, but much faster than usual. This resulted in unusual actions and ideas including thoughts of suicide in my then nine-year-old son. In addition, my son developed a reaction to the antiseizure medication, so the neurologist put him on a different drug. Meanwhile the pediatric psychiatrist put him back on the original antipsychotic drug.

When I first called Deena, my son was having severe mood swings accompanied by emotional outbursts. He had a low tolerance for frustration, and various attention problems, as well as hyperactivity. Deena spoke with my son by phone for a minute and then did a long-distance healing off the phone for about an hour. She told me that she expected the progress to be gradual.

It was gradual, but so pronounced that a few weeks after the initial healing, a long-time next door neighbor and friend said to me, "What happened to your son? He seems so much better." After taking a deep breath, I told her about Deena.

Shortly afterward, I was visiting that same neighbor and a friend of hers at her house. She also remarked on my son's improved behavior. Ever since the healing I have noticed that my son is much smoother. The jerkiness and agitation that he had prior to the healing are completely gone. It really is an amazing difference.

Deena has done a few quick healing balances in the months since the original long session. My son continues to grow calmer and more refined. He no longer takes any medication. Outside stimulus is handled with much more equanimity, and he is a pleasure to be around. Even the doctors noticed the change. I decided not to tell them about Deena for fear they would prescribe a drug for me.

Several months after the intuitive read with Louise and the healing on the boy, I mentioned the entire situation to Marlene, including the information on the energized rock salt and camphor. She told me that three years earlier she had a case where people and their pets had been poisoned by the use of pesticides in a house. Her guides had given her similar information involving rock salt, pure camphor, and energy for activation, in order to detox the house. Neither she nor Louise had ever heard of such a thing. Neither had I. Now *that* is validation!

CHAPTER XVIII

Not Yet Mainstream Medicine

I long for the day when medicine is truly integrative, when all the best of the healing arts are combined to help the patient. While progress is being made, we are a far cry from that world. In earlier chapters, I mentioned situations where information about healings was not, and could not, be shared with doctors, even though it would have helped explain to them why they were witnessing the unexpected.

One example from an earlier chapter was Linda Y., protected by an energy "chemo-cloud" that created harmony in all substances infused in her, and so she had no side effects from her chemotherapy. Although it would have been the absolute best to have timed the making of the "chemocloud" as close as possible to the actual infusion of the chemicals, Linda could not say to her doctor, "Before you start this, let me just give my healer a ring to let her know we are about to begin. And by the way it's a long-distance call. Is that OK?"

The previous chapter told the story of the Dursban-poisoned young man, whose doctors made him increasingly worse by drugging him—multiplying the toxic assaults. They have no idea why he is doing much better now and off all medication. As Linda N., the mother, explained, telling them would probably have resulted in a drug prescription for her. So most patients don't bother talking to their physicians about energy healings (never mind long-distance ones), even though they may have dramatically changed a situation. Why gain nothing but the label of "new-age flake?"

This past year I had the opportunity to participate in an unusual healing. The 36-year-old daughter of a friend of mine was hospitalized with life-threatening infections. The immune system of the young woman was severely depressed because of the drugs she needed to take in order to avoid rejection of a kidney-pancreas transplant from seven years earlier. She was diagnosed at age 10 with diabetes, and by the time she was in her late 20s, her kidneys were failing. The transplanted pancreas resolved the insulin problem of the diabetes, but the antirejection drugs created a suppressed immune system (which is what they are designed to do), making her more susceptible to infection.

At the time I learned of the situation, the doctors were very concerned that my friend's daughter might die; they greatly reduced the antirejection medication in the hope that her immune system would recover enough to ensure her survival. However, they felt that lowering the dosage of the antirejection medicine created a strong possibility that she would reject the transplant. They told her they thought it would be better to lose those organs, than to die.

When the young woman's mother mentioned all of this to me, I offered to try something I had not done before—remove the energy signature of the organ donor and infuse the energy of the young woman into the kidney-pancreas transplant. If successful, the need for high doses of antirejection medicine could, I thought, be lessened or eliminated. (However, I doubted the doctors would ever try eliminating the drug altogether, as that would be totally illogical and could not possibly make sense to them.)

I never spoke with the patient. In fact, in this situation, I did not have the opportunity to get the patient's conscious consent—something I much prefer to do. The daughter didn't and doesn't believe in the sort of work I do. I can't explain why I felt it was all right to go ahead with this healing without consulting the patient at a conscious level, but I just felt certain it was. It was a life and death matter, and in any case if she didn't want the shift in energy, it would not be accepted.

I connected to the daughter's energy field by asking her mother to think of her while we were on the phone. The daughter was hospitalized in a town over a hundred miles away. I tuned into the energy of the deceased organ donor. It was not pretty. I later found out that the donor had been a very troubled young man who was in his late teens or early 20s when he died in a fistfight.

I began to remove his energy from the transplanted organs and infuse the energy of the recipient. Part way through this procedure, I had the opportunity to connect with my guide through Louise Cook. He told me to discontinue the removal of the young man's energy, and to simply infuse the woman's energy, because the donor's energy would then dissolve on its own. I didn't understand the reason for this, but I trusted it and proceeded according to instructions.

The doctors were checking creatinine levels in the blood of their patient on a daily basis. Creatinine is an end stage product of metabolism, which is filtered out of the blood by the kidneys and then excreted into the urine. If the kidneys are failing, they are unable to filter out this waste product, which leaves high levels of creatinine in the blood. Since the young woman was now on a low dose of the antirejection medicine, they expected to see a rise in the creatinine—an indication that the kidney-pancreas transplant was being rejected. But the creatinine did not rise. Instead, immediately after the healing, the creatinine level went down, and it stayed down, indicating improved renal (kidney) function. Not only was the organ not being rejected, it was being better accepted.

My friend wrote the following for this book:

> *The day after Deena completed the healing, I was at the hospital when a puzzled-looking doctor came into my daughter's room. He said that he had gotten the latest test results and not only was the creatinine level down, but it was lower than it had been in the past year. "It must be a fluke," he remarked. But the next day the test revealed the same results. The day after that it was still the same and has been ever since. The doctor had no explanation for this. He never brought it up again.*

I am writing this months later. The dosage of the antirejection medicine has been left at the same lower levels as more has not been needed. The original higher dosage was determined by much experimentation and it had been demonstrated that she could not function with less and still keep her transplanted organs. Clearly something changed.

Wouldn't it be nice if more trained healers and more doctors could work together? I bet some transplants wouldn't require antirejection drugs at all. Will there come a time for this kind of teamwork? I hope so.

As far as I can tell, although I believe I helped resolve one problem, the young woman still has an uphill battle ahead of her. The situation, as I understand it (with help from my guide), is that the young woman has an underlying belief that she is not worthy or important to anyone. This misinterpretation of reality was the original cause of the diabetes, which, step-by-step, led to various medical complications and ultimately the transplant.

Unfortunately, her belief has not changed, which is what is needed for the young woman to fully regain her health and live a long life. Although she is much beloved by her family, including her husband, as long as her thinking remains as it is she cannot truly accept that she is valued. Understanding that there is a mental cause that has brought about, and keeps her in, ill health is not an easy task. And even if she begins to search for healing at deeper levels, making such profound changes is no small feat. However, I believe she can do it if she chooses.

CHAPTER XIX

Heart of an Angel

If you can start the day without caffeine,
if you can get along without pep pills,
if you can always be cheerful, ignoring aches and pains,
if you can resist complaining and boring people with your troubles,
if you can eat the same food every day and be grateful for it,
if you can understand when your loved ones are too busy to give you any time,
if you can overlook it when those you love take it out on you when,
    through no fault of yours, something goes wrong,
if you can take criticism and blame without resentment,
if you can ignore a friend's limited education and never correct him/her,
if you can resist treating a rich friend better than a poor friend,
if you can face the world without lies and deceit,
if you can conquer tension without medical help,
if you can relax without liquor,
if you can sleep without the aid of drugs,
if you can honestly say that deep in your heart you have
    no prejudice against creed, color, religion, or politics,

Then, my friend, you are ALMOST as good as your dog.

I don't know the author of this piece, which was sent to me by e-mail. I think it is the perfect introduction to a chapter about the energy healing and the healing energy of animals. They are such wonderful beings.

Illness in animals has many causes, and, as with humans, sometimes the energy sent to them for healing is accepted and sometimes it is not. When an animal chooses to be healed, on occasion the results can be dramatic. Such was the case with Brodie, a two-and-a-half-year-old dog who graces the home of Ann M. in Alexandria, Virginia. Ann initially e-mailed me the following:

> *. . . Brodie, however, has continued to have ear problems, so much so that I recently had a vet look at him. The vet indicated that Brodie has a severe ear infection with a good bit of scar tissue. I am going to do what I need to do to keep his ears clean and use the medication provided by the vet, but I wondered if it was possible for you to also help him. I have a feeling that the ear infection may only be a symptom of something else—the vet wasn't sure. He's only two years old and that's kinda young to have such an ear problem. The vet seemed to think that the scar tissue would be permanent, and that if it worsened he might have to have surgery. I have this fundamental distrust of the scalpel and wanted to try everything else first. I would so much appreciate it if you could help him. He is such a sweet boy! Let me know what you think . . . Ann M.*

Ann sent me a picture of her dog and we arranged a time for a long-distance session, which we began on the phone. I asked Ann to think of Brodie so I could connect with his auric field. The energy around Brodie's ears felt blocked. I worked for about an hour, at first on his entire field and then specifically on the obstruction in and around his ears. By the end of the session, Brodie's energy field felt like it was flowing nicely and had the felt-sound of a deep and resonant violin.

I also performed a quick "tune-up" on the rest of the members of the family—human and animal. I find it is better to have as much harmony surrounding a client as possible because it increases the chances that a healing will take place and will hold. Something must have been right because less than 24 hours later, it was as if Brodie had exchanged his damaged ears for a healthy new set. I received the following e-mail:

> *I just wanted to say thank you soooo much for your help! Dr. A indicated that we would not be able to eliminate the scar tissue (short of surgery) or the leathery/elephantine texture of the skin from Brodie's ears. He also said that it would be some time before we eliminated the odor from his ears. On Saturday morning I checked his ears and the leathery/elephantine texture was gone and his ears were smooth again. The odor was also significantly reduced and I could feel the difference at the base of the ear. I could not believe the overnight change in his ears. Moreover, he seems to be back to his playful self. Thank you. The change is so amazing!*

As I began to write the story of Brodie for this chapter, I e-mailed Ann for further comments or updates. She recalled that the vet, in addition to saying that the only way the scar tissue could be eliminated was by surgery, had also indicated that the scar tissue deep inside the ears could worsen with time, requiring surgery to preserve Brodie's hearing. His earflaps today (many months later) remain "baby smooth" and "subsequent exams by the vet have indicated that there is no longer scar tissue inside his ears."

It is definitely gratifying to witness a "miraculous" recovery. We are supposed to let go of the outcome, but I love both helping someone get well and having such clear validation of my healing work. OK, there I said it; I hope that doesn't sign me up for another two thousand years of incarnation to get over it.

No matter how much energy a healer attempts to send, there are times when nothing, or little, changes. In the case of one cat who had heart problems, I ignored my guidance and kept trying to get the energy through for about an hour. The cat's human was so distraught, and I empathized with her feelings so much I just kept sending energy, even though I felt little progress and possibly resistance. I knew better, but I did it anyway. Eventually the cat's field budged—slightly. Very slightly, but slightly. I was completely exhausted for the rest of the day and evening. I called Louise Cook for assistance. She translated for my guide: "The cat doesn't give a damn." (I have never heard Louise, a dainty and delicate lady, use such language.) I inquired if the energy I had expended had been a total waste. My guide responded that the cat had used a "little" of it, but, he added, "Don't do that again."

I called the human with this news and my experience of the healing. She confirmed that the description sounded just like her cat's personality. That's part of what they loved about her. When next I spoke with the cat's family, I learned after the healing that the cat, Liebchen, had become much more "clubby" and willing to honor them briefly with her presence. She also seemed less agitated. The day after the healing, Liebchen lay down in front of the refrigerator and peacefully died. It was her plan all along. She has since been spotted sitting on a rock in "summerland" (the name given to the dimension where spirits go between earth lives) with not a care in the world.

When it is difficult to effect a change in an animal's condition, it might be because the animal is reflecting something from and for the human companion. One example was a cat who urinated on the carpets only if both humans were home. It was her comment on the energy of the relationship between the two humans, which she confirmed in a telepathic exchange with animal communicator Terri Diener.

In another case, a dog became temporarily blind immediately after his human's boyfriend yelled at the sensitive canine. After that, the dog had various problems with his eyesight, but I could feel him resisting the healing energy that I was sending. The "read" from several intuitives was that the human was having trouble "seeing" the reality of the relationship between herself and her boyfriend. The dog was her guidance.

Sophia is a wonderful cat who lives with my friends, Tom and Jill. Sophia became diabetic, but each time I tried to send healing to her, I felt an extraordinarily beautiful energy coming back to me. Sophia seemed to be saying, "Thank you very much, but I don't need it." The intuitive "read" (from Carla Gordan) indicated that the diabetes was a "reflection" of Jill, who was not in an emotionally satisfying work environment and could not allow her own sweetness out. (Diabetes usually has some connection to a lack of sweetness in life.) Once Jill became aware of her role in her cat's illness, she followed the guidance and took steps to make changes in her professional situation. After that, Sophia's health improved to the point where she no longer needed insulin shots. My job was to send energy to Jill; her cat had no use for it.

There are plenty of cases in which an animal is simply ready to die and will either not accept any healing energy or will use it to ease and hasten a departure. Many times an animal in an older body wants to leave quickly, so he or she can return in a new, younger fur costume. To the animals, leaving and returning again to physical life is no big deal—it is just the acquisition of a new outfit. They are far more consciously connected to spirit than most of us humans are.

We had a wonderful frog, "Gerard," who lived in a small man-made pond outside our front door in Maryland. This was a very unusual frog, with obvious personality. He appeared to be a very confident, happy being who allowed me to approach and sit next to him. One unusually cold winter, the entire tiny pond became a block of ice. I discovered Gerard's frozen, lifeless form. Devastated, I phoned Marlene, who had communicated with him in the past. Gerard, perfectly happy as always, was right there when she tuned in, "We don't have your neurotic attachment to death," he said.

Gerard

CHAPTER XX

An Ancient 23rd Century Art

SO FAR TODAY I'VE DONE ALL RIGHT.
I HAVEN'T GOSSIPED.
I HAVEN'T LOST MY TEMPER.
I HAVEN'T BEEN GREEDY, GRUMPY, NASTY, SELFISH, NOR SELF-INDULGENT.
I'M VERY THANKFUL FOR THAT.
HOWEVER, IN A FEW MOMENTS I'M GOING TO GET OUT OF BED,
AND FROM THEN ON I'M GOING TO NEED A LOT OF HELP.

The above gem has been in the notebook of my friend Marianne for decades, but she doesn't remember if she wrote it or someone else did. We both agree it is a worthy piece.

If one wants to become an energy healer, a very important part of one's lifetime task is to work on one's own character. Healing is at least as much about learning one's own issues, wounds, and defenses as it is about learning techniques. It's a good idea to lighten your own load before imagining you can help anyone else. It's also desirable to not inflict your problems on your client.

Most professions don't include personal work as an equal part of the training. If healers are not working from their hearts, and if they are not centered and grounded, they are not performing healings. A surgeon in a bad mood can successfully cut open a heart and replace a damaged valve, but a healer is helping to replace something that runs deeper than a damaged valve—a damaged spirit, which can lead to a physically impaired heart. A healer who truly intends to be of service doesn't have the luxury of being crabby or having an inflated ego in his or her work with clients.

Another reason healers need to stay centered, grounded, and in our hearts is because many of us are on the scene a little early for the adoration of the general population. If you want to be a healer, it is important to realize that in this day and age you will hardly enjoy the respect of a doctor: *"Oh, my daughter married a healer! I am so thrilled!"* I don't think so.

I also don't expect that any time soon people will be compiling records of bills paid to their healers so that they can be deducted on their tax returns, or reimbursed by their medical insurance companies. In fact, we often enjoy the same lack of respect that some of the great composers, such as Beethoven and Brahms, received from their critics when their music was first introduced. This was true even though part of the public loved their work.

The Lexicon of Musical Invective—Critical Assaults on Composers since Beethoven's Time by Nicolas Slonimsky, is a treasure trove of examples of what Slonimsky calls "non-acceptance of the unfamiliar." "In dance, art, literature, and in politics, the psychological phenomenon of Non-acceptance of the Unfamiliar operates as forcefully as in music." Slonimsky gives examples of vitriolic criticism of new musical instruments: "We have a machine which in the baritone register suggests a cow in dyspeptic distress." He offers a sample of medical mudslinging with commentary of Pasteur who discovered a connection between microbes and illness: "It is absurd to think," declared Dr. Nicolas Joly of Toulouse, "that germs causing fermentation and putrefaction came from the air; the atmosphere would have to be as thick as pea soup for that." (If Dr. Joly lived now, treated as we are to the comfort of sometimes seeing the air we breathe—and indeed it can be thick and pea-soup-colored—he might want to rethink his argument.)

Personal work is required in order to channel the most loving and effective healing energy. The increased strength of character it brings may also be needed to weather what may be more than a lifetime (how convenient that we have extras) of detractors. I have no problem with a skeptical mind, so long as it's open enough to honestly evaluate the possible genuineness of an unexplained matter, should a truth be placed in front of it. However, threatening the view of some folks' reality can create an explosive (and in retrospect, amusing) response. I cannot resist giving some additional colorful examples from Slonimsky's book. Healers will definitely need to keep their senses of humor dusted off:

. . . delivered by W.C. Brann of Waco, Texas, against a newspaper editor: "I can but wonder what will become of the editor of the Los Angeles Times *when the breath leaves his feculent body and death stops the rattling of his abortive brain. He cannot be buried in the sea lest he poison the fishes. He cannot be suspended in mid-air, like Mahomet's coffin, lest the circling worlds, in their endeavor to avoid contamination, crash together, wreck the universe and bring about the return of chaos and Old Night. The damn scoundrel is a white elephant on the hands of the Deity, and I have some curiosity to know what He will do with him."*

It is difficult to top the passionate prose of the above excerpt, but I'd like to quote a few more examples to remind the sympathetic reader that it's OK to laugh if they come across something less than complimentary concerning those who practice the art of energy healing. It may also be helpful to remember that perspectives change; what is written now may later reveal more about the commentator than the subject at hand, just as these reviews do. Meanwhile, I'm not expecting any awards for my work or this book.

From *The Lexicon of Musical Invective* on Beethoven:

We find Beethoven's Ninth Symphony to be precisely one hour and five minutes long: a fearful period indeed, which puts the muscles and lungs of the band, and the patience of the audience to a severe trial. . . . The last movement, a chorus, is heterogeneous. What relation it bears to the symphony we could not make out; and here, as well as in other parts, the want of intelligible design is too apparent.

(The Harmonicon, *London, April 1825*)

The merits of Beethoven's Seventh Symphony we have before discussed, and we repeat, that . . . it is a composition in which the author has indulged a great deal of disagreeable eccentricity. Often as we now have heard it performed, we cannot yet discover any design in it, neither can we trace any connection in its parts. Altogether, it seems to have been intended as a kind of enigma—we had almost said a hoax.

(The Harmonicon, *London, July 1825*)

And a couple of whacks at Johannes Brahms, the first one translated from the German language:

> *The second number was Brahms's Piano Concerto in B-flat major, played by the composer himself. Who can swallow this concerto with appetite, can calmly await a famine; it is to be assumed that he enjoys an enviable digestion, and in time of famine will be able to get along splendidly on the nutritive equivalent of window glass, cork stoppers, stove pipes, and the like.*
>
> *(Hugo Wolf,* Salonblatt, *Vienna, December 13, 1884)*

> *. . . It must be admitted that to the larger part of our public, Brahms is still an incomprehensible terror.*
>
> (Boston Evening Transcript, *November 16, 1885)*

Substitute the words "energy healing" in place of "Brahms" in that last review and now we are up to date.

CHAPTER XXI

This Must Be the Last Chapter: I'm Out of Chips

"Too much spiritual evolution takes all the pleasure out of being negative."

This probably should be the follow-up line to *be careful, you might get what you wish for.* Helping yourself or someone else to heal physically, ultimately involves spiritual healing. Matter is created from spirit. An unhappy self creates unhappy matter. The question is: how do we live more healthfully and happily in the so-called "real" world? Perhaps we should instead call it "the world of physical matter" as the word "real" is subject to debate. (It's inconvenient to have an argument with a consciousness focused in another reality who considers *you* a figment of the imagination and themselves real, thank you very much.)

Yes, a big key to healing yourself is to love yourself. Fine, but most people truly do not. So what can be done to change this situation? What if you know you want to change, but are struggling? The key is so simple that it is elusive. It is just now dawning on me, although there are some people who have always known it. It came by way of a painful emotional episode, that old conduit of learning I keep wishing would become outdated; or perhaps it is, but no one has pulled it off my shelf.

Someone close to me yelled at me in an uncharacteristic way with accusations that just stunned me. Unfairly, unjustly, blah, blah, blah. I was hurt, I was angry, but I also knew that each of us creates our own multi-act play here. I created this unpleasantness? Darn. But why?

I really wanted to feel sorry for myself and take "poor me" out of retirement, but the negative pleasure of "poor me" had lost some of its allure. It wouldn't make me feel better anymore. If I wanted to continue in my own spiritual growth, I'd have to find pleasure elsewhere.

I sort of understood that I had authored the incident to show myself that it was time to work on self-love and self-trust. I was still having trouble with these skills. There was great temptation to blame the offending party, instead of keeping the focus on the scene as my creation, my script.

In my discomfort, I certainly was giving this bit of writing a "D minus." What the heck class had I missed? Sure I didn't always make all the early morning ones, but I was pretty good about attending the rest of them. What was I not getting?

My right ear plugged up. "OK! OK! I know I'm not hearing something," I thought with growing frustration and anguish. What is the key to self-love, the key to living in this strange world of tax returns and tanning salons, a dimension and place we have created to teach unconditional love? It's just so simple it escapes most of us. It's *no expectations.* That's it. No expectations.

If you depend and rely on yourself for doing the things you can do, and depend on yourself for love, whatever anyone else does that's kind, helpful, and loving is a gift. If the hot water comes out of the hot water tap when you turn it on, it's a gift. If your car starts, it's a gift. If your dog wags his tail when he sees you, it's a gift. If you expect love or something done for you from others and they don't comply, then you have brought hurt and disappointment upon yourself. That is not self-love.

This applies to expectation of yourself as well. Most people have an idealized version of themselves and they simply do not measure up to it. Since they cannot accept themselves as they are, they do not love themselves. This does not mean that you do not strive to evolve—to become more loving. It means you accept yourself and other beings as they are and don't expect anything better or worse.

You have preferences, certainly. In healing and in life, you picture what you'd like with loving intent and without trying to control another's behavior. Then let go of the picture—no expectations. Doing this frees the energy, allowing for better flow and more harmony.

You are not required to continue associating with someone who is not in harmony with you. If the best they can do is too often not compatible with your happiness and health, immersing yourself in their energy field is not self-love either.

I see a relationship between the concept of no expectations and the definition of forgiveness as I learned it from Carla Gordan during a reading for a client. Forgiveness is not saying that someone did something lousy, rotten, and no good; however, I am releasing the prisoner. That is still judgment. It is understanding that the person, no matter how offensive the behavior, did the very best they could in that moment; otherwise they would have done it differently. It is making that true for yourself as well. Few of us are used to thinking this way, myself included.

If you have no expectations, then actually there is never a need to forgive anyone. If we remember that we wrote the play and every line in it, and we do not have expectations, then we will not be affected in the same way if someone behaves like a rabid dragon. We won't take it personally. Picture harmony around yourself. This frees you, and this frees them.

Not having expectations of ourselves does not mean that we are excused from our own poor behavior. It means that we acknowledge a lackluster performance, make amends, and know we would have done better in that moment if we could have. Drowning in guilt is not a plus (I know. I know! That goes against my heritage), and doesn't lead to self-love, either. Having recognized that our actions (or thoughts) didn't feel good, we can set our intention to have more grace in the next moment.

Setting our intention to evolve is different from "expecting" we will conduct ourselves perfectly next time. The latter can lead to feelings of failure if we don't emulate our impossible model, giving us more reason to hate ourselves. This creates more dissonant energy, which in turn attracts more discordant energy, and our planet grows increasingly cacophonous and off-key.

If you beat yourself over the head for every wrong note when learning to play an instrument, you won't advance musically, and all you'll have to show for your efforts is a sorry-looking, squashed cranium. Life, I think, is much the same; it is best to accept that you are in book two of your lessons and not expect to be ready to play a concerto by the end of the semester. Intend to continue improving. Give yourself a gold star as you finish each book. It is good to remember we are after wholeness, not perfection.

Have I dropped expectations yet? Well no. Do I expect to? Ha! I did read what I just typed and I'm not going there. I'm just learning about it too, but I'm setting my intention to at least lower my expectations (not to be confused with lowering my standards) as a start. I may have to take this step by step. Whatever of this new state I have mustered feels like a weight lifted off me. It assists in letting go of the hurts in our memory banks and helps avoid the creation of more pain for ourselves.

People are messy. Thankfully, most individuals strive for good acts, but because of their own fears fall short at times. The point here is that it is important to *love the essence* of every being while having no expectations about the behavior of anyone temporarily in physical pajamas in a particular moment in time.

Having no expectations enables us to love those who seem to be unlovable, no matter what they may have done. They need it. It enables us to love ourselves. We need it. We are much more than our achievements and our misachievements. (If the government can make up words, I can too.) In the end, healing is not some impersonal technique of running energy. What heals is love. Our essence is love, and it is who we really are. The rest is just insanity, but it's only temporary.

Healings and Workshops with Deena Spear:

If you are interested in having healings or taking workshops with Deena you can contact her through her website: www. singing-woods.org or obtain information by calling her recording at 607 387-8488.

Workshops will be offered:
- For anyone interested in learning more conscious awareness of energy in physical and non-physical reality.
- For beginning and advanced students of healing.
- For people who are in the performance arts, such as singers, instrumentalists, dancers, actors, and speakers. Programs will include healing and grounding work.
- Workshops can be tailored to the wishes of a particular group.
- For violin makers interested in learning to perform the innovative physical acoustics described in Part II of the hardbound version of *Ears of the Angels*.

To contact the intuitives/healers mentioned in this book:

Marlene Sandler: Intuitive Counseling, Animal Communication, Healing.
215 918-0692 (Fax: 215 491-0202)
P.O. Box 476, Warrington, PA 18976-0476

Louise Cook: Connection to angel guides.
By individual referral from Deena.

Roberta Herzog: Akashic Record Reading (past/simultaneous life information).
P.O. Box 20188, Greenville, NC 27858

Terri Diener: Animal Communication.
410 358-3954
www.petspeak.com

Carla Gordan: Full-trance medium/ teacher of heart-centered living.
By individual referral from Deena.

Carol Kulig: Healing.
212 662-7998
carol@paragenesis.com

To contact the artist **Bruce Burgess:**
Write to him at 862 Queenstown Road, Lancaster, VA 22503

We hope you enjoyed this Hay House book.
If you would like to receive a free catalog featuring additional
Hay House books and products, or if you would like information about the
Hay Foundation, please contact:

Hay House, Inc.
P.O. Box 5100
Carlsbad, CA 92018-5100

(760) 431-7695 or **(800) 654-5126**
(760) 431-6948 (fax) or **(800) 650-5115 (fax)**
www.hayhouse.com

Published and distributed in Australia by:
Hay House Australia Pty Ltd, 18/36 Ralph St., Alexandria NSW 2015
Phone: 612-9669-4299 • *Fax:* 612-9669-4144 • *E-mail:* info@hayhouse.com.au

Published and Distributed in the United Kingdom by:
Hay House UK, Ltd. • Unit 202, Canalot Studios • 222 Kensal Rd., London W10 5BN
Phone: 020-8962-1230 • *Fax:* 020-8962-1239

Distributed in Canada by:
Raincoast • 9050 Shaughnessy St., Vancouver, B.C. V6P 6E5
Phone: (604) 323-7100 • *Fax:* (604) 323-2600